Jubilee CELEBRATIONS #2

Bertha M. Landers

Brethren Press

The development of *Jubilee Celebrations 2* was made possible through a grant from Schowalter Foundation, Inc., Newton, Kansas.

This publication uses the New Revised Standard Version of the Bible, copyright © 1989, by the Division of Christian Education of the National Council of Churches of Christ in the U.S.A. Used by permission.

Cover design by Merrill Miller

99 98 97 96 95   5 4 3 2 1

Library of Congress Cataloging-in-Publication Data

(Revised for vol. 2)

Harnish, Dorothy M., 1941–
    Jubilee celebrations.

    Includes bibliographical references.
    1. Worship programs. I. Title.
BV198.H37 1994   264   93-43573
ISBN 0-87178-477-7 (pbk. : v. 1)
ISBN 0-87178-475-0 (pbk. : v. 2)

Printed in the United States of America

Contents

The Spirit of the Lord is upon me,
  because he has anointed me
    to bring good news to the poor.
He has sent me to proclaim release to the captives
    and recovery of sight to the blind,
    to let the oppressed go free,
to proclaim the year of the Lord's favor.

—Luke 4:18-19

Preface

Jesus spoke to them in parables saying, "The kingdom of heaven may be compared to a king who gave a wedding banquet for his son."

Matthew 22:2

Imagine! The kingdom of heaven is a wedding reception! It is a time to sing and dance, a time to laugh and make music, a time to dress up and celebrate, a time when no one is a stranger or foreigner, a time to look forward to something totally new, a time to party! From where did the notion arise that to become a Christian is to forsake all joy and vitality and celebration?

As family celebrations of birthdays, holidays, and milestones enrich and strengthen the family, so celebrations in the church family deepen the fellowship and joy and spiritual vitality of the congregation. When we look at the story of the children of Israel and wonder how God was able to preserve this small band of people, one of the observations we cannot fail to note is that they celebrated together. There were ten major feasts or festivals. The Feast of Unleavened Bread lasted seven days. The Feast of Tabernacles required the building of "summer camp" and camping out. The name alone of the Feast of Trumpets called for celebration.

Celebration was so important in Hebrew life and faith that the children of Israel were told to set aside a tithe for this purpose. "Set apart a tithe of all the yield of your seed that is brought in yearly from the field. . . . And you shall eat there in the presence of the Lord your God, you and your household rejoicing together" (Deut. 14:22-26).

These celebrations were a foretaste of the kingdom to come. Jesus, the messenger of the kingdom of God, participated regularly in them. In fact, it was during the festival of the Passover in the last hours of Jesus' life that he reveals God's plan for him and the world. From that moment, the Passover celebration of deliverance and salvation took on a fresh meaning for the followers of Jesus. They no longer celebrated what had happened in the past. Now they celebrated with anticipation the things that were to come. Two thousand years later we still celebrate the promise. Let the celebrations continue!

—*Bertha M. Landers*

Introduction

How to use this book

These celebrations are for the whole church and require cooperation between pastors, worship committees, and education committees. The first item of business is to set up a meeting of key people from each group to plan a celebration. Then use the following list as an agenda.

1. Pick a date for your celebration and begin planning at least eight weeks ahead.

2. Plan for a 1½- to 2-hour time period to celebrate. Dispense with the regular worship time and Sunday school time. The celebration will accomplish both. Allow 30-45 minutes in each celebration for activities.

3. Modify. These celebrations were written for the typical church with a sanctuary, fellowship hall, and classrooms, an active Sunday school, and a multi-talented membership. If this doesn't describe your congregation, modify the plan to fit your people and facilities.

4. Activities are designed for school-age children through adults. Provide your usual care for preschoolers, infants, and toddlers.

5. Permission is granted, unless indicated otherwise, to reproduce prayers, litanies, and music in worship bulletins, provided that no part of such reproduction is sold or distributed beyond the event held in the local church and provided that proper credit is given to the original author.

6. If suggested hymns are unfamiliar, replace them with hymns from your congregation's hymnal or songbooks.

7. Invite guest speakers early to avoid schedule conflicts, and allow them plenty of time to prepare.

8. Assign leaders, musicians, and teachers in advance. They will need time to gather supplies, rehearse, and prepare presentations. Materials for activities are too numerous to include in the "You will need" section. Urge activity leaders to read their instructions early and gather all necessary items, remembering that in many cases participants will come to the activity centers in shifts.

9. To help you prepare, a sample bulletin is provided in each celebration. You may wish to include information that is specific to your event, such as hymn choices and locations of activity centers.

10. Brief instructions for activities are included in each celebration. Leaders may need to expand activities or try them out ahead of time to ensure smooth sailing on the day of the celebration. In very large congregations, duplicate activity centers to accommodate more people in small groups. Be prepared to direct people to the location of each activity center.

11. Several celebrations suggest a topic for a sermon or homily. The pastor may use the suggested topic or create a new one. Or the planning committee may decide to use an alternative to the sermon, such as a videotape or drama.

12. Promote the celebration four weeks ahead of time on posters and in church newsletters, bulletins, the newspaper religion section, and Sunday school handouts.

13. Many of the music resources suggested in *Jubilee Celebrations 2* are found in *Hymnal: A Worship Book.* The hymnal can be ordered from either Brethren Press (1451 Dundee Avenue, Elgin, IL 60120, 800 441-3712), Faith and Life Press (Box 347, Newton KS, 67114-0347, 800 743-2484), or Mennonite Publishing House (616 Walnut Avenue, Scottdale, PA 15683-1999, 800 245-7894).

The options for use of *Jubilee* celebrations are unlimited. Some congregations will find that Sunday evening worship, retreats, midweek services, or holiday programs are more appropriate times for *Jubilee* celebrations. Planning committees may wish to use portions of these celebrations for other occasions, and variation is possible and encouraged. Whatever form a celebration takes, it should uphold the philosophy of *Jubilee Celebrations,* whose intent is to unify children and adults, worship and nurture.

About the author

Bertha Landers has been an elementary school teacher and a pastor in the Mennonite Church. With a particular interest in drama, she has written plays for children's worship as well as chancel dramas for a traveling drama troop which she led. Bertha lives in Waterloo, Ontario, where she received her M.Div., from Waterloo Lutheran Seminary. She is now retired—"in a manner of speaking."

I Love to Tell the Story

Celebrate Passing on the Faith

The essential expression of Christian love is, in its roots, the commandment to transmit the teaching.

—Jacob Needleman

Moses is about to die. The children of Israel are going to begin a new life in a new land. They are at the threshold of a new chapter in their history. They are out of the wilderness but they are without a leader. Perhaps many of them doubted that they could survive as a people; it did not look promising. Have you ever wondered how this small band of peoples survived and maintained their spiritual center? The answer lies in the fact that they followed God's instruction to pass on the faith. Perhaps you heard the often repeated prediction that the church will not survive very far into the future. As we begin this new year in the life of the church, we are given a fresh opportunity and responsibility to pass on the faith.

Bible Text

Deuteronomy 6:4-9, 20-25; Psalm 78:1-4; 2 Timothy 1:3-7

Bible Background for Our Celebration

Deuteronomy contains Moses' farewell speech to the Hebrews as they prepare to enter Canaan. The great leader Moses made the arduous journey to the edge of the promised land, but he would not get there with the Hebrew people. Knowing he could not enter Canaan, he gave the people instructions for carrying on the faith. If they follow the instructions, Moses tells them in Deuteronomy 6, things will go well between them and their God. Children will have faith. If they keep the commandments, their days will be long. Moreover, the people of God will "multiply greatly in the land flowing with milk and honey, as the Lord, the God of your ancestors, has promised you." Most importantly, the people will want to follow these instructions simply out of gratitude for God's love and promises.

Deuteronomy 6:4-9 is known as the Shema, which is Hebrew for "hear" or "listen." The Shema is a basic creedal statement in Judaism to this day, instructing the Hebrews in the faith. First, the Shema states who God is and the relationship of the people to God (v. 4). Then Moses tells how the people are to honor God. Whereas the first three verses of the chapter tell how the people will benefit from their faithful relationship with God, verses 4-9 tell how God will benefit from the honor and devotion of the people.

"Hear, O Israel" is a call to attention. It is used many times in

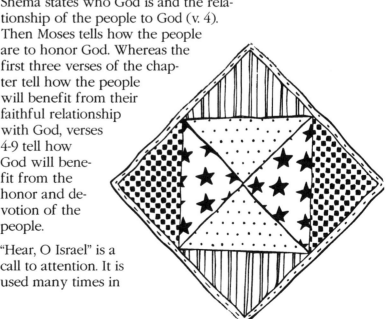

Deuteronomy to announce that a solemn and important message is to follow. This call summons us to listen and to hear with the inner ear. These words are addressed to the community as a whole and to each listener. It speaks to the relationships of God and Israel (v. 4), of Moses and Israel (v. 6), and of parents and children (v. 7).

"When your children ask" (vv. 20-22) is followed by an old confession of faith. The Israelites realized that a confession of faith in abstract terms was not enough. The children were to learn about faith through the story of God's creative and redemptive acts. Of course, the most outstanding one for them was the deliverance from slavery and the gift of the promised land. The gift of the law was not a burden to be borne but an act of God's grace and love. By following these laws, the Israelites would live life more abundantly. The statutes were to be handed down not as dull dogma, but as dramatic examples of true faith from their very own ancestors. These stories inspired faith in the next generation.

Singing and repeating the Psalms helped to keep the story alive and fresh for Hebrews and Christians. Psalm 78, for example, is a recital of Israel's salvation history from the time of Jacob to David that may have been recited at festivals such as the Passover. Its aim is to show how God has been working in and through Israel's history. As we sing hymns of history and faith with our children at home and in various settings, their faith and lives are being shaped, like the lives of Hebrew children.

The story of Timothy is an example of how faith is shared in the home. Timothy was the son of a Greek father and Jewish mother. He was nurtured in the faith by his grandmother and his mother. Their early attention to his training in the faith made it possible for Paul to invite young Timothy to accompany him on his missionary journey. They exemplify that not only the stories of our ancestors and their faith form our belief, but also that the more modern stories of our own parents' faith inspire us—perhaps more so.

Faith Nugget

Faith comes to us not only in a personal relationship with God, but through the community that raises us and passes on the faith.

Early Preparation

Ask the worship leader and faith center leaders to meet several weeks in advance. Go over the entire worship service together. Choose the location for each center. Have the supplies in place before the worship service begins.

For the Message time in the celebration, ask several members two or three weeks ahead of time to prepare to share their story of how they came to faith or how they teach their faith. Ask them to think about the people who shared their faith with them, who taught them, and were models and mentors.

You will need
- ☐ copies of the bulletin for the celebration
- ☐ index cards and pencils
- ☐ symbols of the faith story
- ☐ old pictures
- ☐ video tapes
- ☐ books and newspaper articles
- ☐ a globe
- ☐ a copy of *The Keeping Quilt* by Patricia Polacco

Name of your church
I Love to Tell the Story
Celebrate Passing on the Faith

Call to Worship

Invocation

Hymns of Praise............. "Holy God,
We Praise Thy Name"
"The God of Abraham, Praise"

Prayer of Confession

Silent Reflection

Assurance of Pardon

Anthem........ "We Would Extol Thee"

Time with the Children.... *The Keeping
Quilt*

Scripture...... Deuteronomy 6:4-9, 20-25
Psalm 78:1-4
2 Timothy 1:3-7

Message................. A Good Story

Hymn Interlude......... "I Love to Tell
the Story"

Faith Centers
1. Learn the Shema. All ages will learn
Deuteronomy 6:4-9 in a variety of
ways.

2. Make Reminders. Make a *mezuzah*
to remind you of the presence of
God.
3. When Your Children Ask. Youth will
pose the hard questions to adults
and ask for answers.
4. Teens Teach Kids. Youth help
younger children learn about God.
5. Tell the Story Through Art. Make
"stained glass" pictures of God's story.
6. Write Your Story. Reflect on paper
how you learned about faith.
7. Tell Your Story. Youth and adults tell
their stories of faith to each other.
8. Sing the Story. Sing the hymns and
songs that tell the story of Jesus.

Gathering Hymns ..... "Two Fishermen"
"Blessed Assurance"
"Lord of the Dance"

Sharing Our Stories

Pastoral Prayer

Offering

Prayer of Dedication

Litany of Commitment and Faith

Hymn of Commission .... "Go, My
Children"

Benediction

The Celebration

As people enter, give them instructions in the bulletin to silently reflect about the many people who have taught them about faith or modeled it for them. Encourage them to use the gathering time to meditate on these people and their influence. If their mentor is present, suggest that they jot a note of appreciation on an index card to him or her.

At the center of the worship area, display old pictures, video tapes, books, a globe, newspaper articles of Christian acts of faith, and other symbols of the faith story.

Call to Worship

One: Hear, O people.

Attend with your inner ear!

The Lord is our God, the Lord alone.

God has done glorious deeds and mighty wonders.

All: We come as the people of God.

Right side: We come as a people with a history.

Left side: We come as a people with a future.

Right side: We come to hear the story.

Left side: We come for we are a part of the story.

All: Come, let us worship God.

Invocation

Gracious God, you have called us to be your people. You have kept your promise to walk with us on our journey. We come now to hear again the old story. We come to hear anew the old story. We come to hear the story for our lives. We come to hear your new words for us.

Rekindle within us the flame that enables us to love you with all our heart, with all our soul, with all our mind. Make yourself known to us afresh, and accept our worship, we pray. Amen.

Hymns of Praise

"Holy God, We Praise Thy Name" (*Te Deum laudamus*), "The God of Abraham, Praise" (Jewish Doxology/Hebrew melody), or other hymn of praise

Prayer of Confession (in unison)

God of all generations, we confess that we have not always loved you with our whole heart and mind and soul. We confess when our actions have not expressed your love. We confess when we have lacked the courage to tell of your gracious deeds. We confess that, unlike Lois and Eunice, we have not always shared your story. Hear our prayer, O God, and forgive us.

Silent Reflection

Assurance of Pardon

God has cared enough to call us to be God's people. God has cared enough to journey with us. God's actions in the world remind us that we are never forsaken. We are forgiven. Hear this good news, rejoice and begin anew!

Anthem

"We Would Extol Thee" (Grieve) or other anthem of adoration

Time with the Children

The Keeping Quilt by Patricia Polacco

Scripture

Deuteronomy 6:4-9, 20-25; Psalm 78:1-4; 2 Timothy 1:3-7

The scripture may be mimed by a family or other group during the reading. For the Deuteronomy passage, mimes can lie down, sit up, and go to bed. For the Timothy passage, Eunice and Lois can pose as if teaching Timothy.

Message

A Good Story

Ask some of the members of the congregation to tell stories of how they pass on the faith to their children. Ask people of various ages to tell how it was passed on to them. If a family is working on learning scripture passages in their home, they may want to recite a passage they have learned. Also ask if someone would like to tell about a situation when they regretted that they had no one to tell them of their faith story.

Hymn Interlude

"I Love to Tell the Story"

Tell the congregation that they will sing the hymn once where they are standing. Then they will sing the entire hymn again as they move out to the faith centers. Use no accompaniment the second time through, and encourage people to hum if they do not know the words. Or reproduce the words of this public domain hymn in the bulletin.

Faith Centers

1. Learn the Shema. This group will use various ways to memorize the Shema (Deut. 6:4-9). Participants may want to try more than one of these ways of memorizing the passage.

a. Read the whole text together from a flip chart that has been made up in advance. Repeat, but rely less and less on the chart.

b. Divide into four groups. Read the text from the flip chart as a choral reading:

> **One voice:** [*loudly*] Hear, O Israel:
>
> **Group 1:** The Lord is our God,
>
> **All:** the Lord alone.
>
> **Group 2:** You shall love the Lord your God

> **Group 3:** with all your heart,
>
> **Group 1:** and with all your soul,
>
> **Group 4:** and with all your might.
>
> **One:** Keep these words that I am commanding you today in your heart.
>
> **Group 2:** Recite them to your children and talk about them when you are at home
>
> **Group 1:** and when you are away,
>
> **Group 3:** when you lie down and when you rise.
>
> **Group 4:** Bind them as a sign on your hand,
>
> **Group 2:** fix them as an emblem on your forehead,
>
> **Group 1:** and write them on the doorposts of your house and on your gates.
>
> **All:** Hear, O Israel: The Lord is our God, the Lord alone.

c. Put the text on flash cards. Mix these. Have groups take turns putting them in the correct order without looking at the Bible.

d. Ask one or more people in the group to compose a simple tune for the text. Learn it together.

e. On one large sheet of sturdy paper, print the passage with words and pictures. Have the children draw and color the picture (for example, an ear to illustrate "hear").

f. Say the text as a rap or a chant.

2. Make Reminders. Make a modern day *mezuzah* in which to keep a copy of the Shema. A mezuzah is a small scroll that Jews sometimes tied to the forehead and left arm. The scroll contained passages of scripture. A modern mezuzah might be a key chain, a plaque for the home or bedroom, the back of a purse mirror, a decorative door knob cover, or a sticker with the scripture on it.

3. When Your Children Ask. Youth will compose a list of faith questions of importance to them and give them to the adults in the group. The adults will take the questions and prepare answers in the form of stories, recalling how Jesus answered questions with a story. Come back together to share the questions and answers.

Some questions youth might ask are: How does scripture that is thousands of years old have anything to say to me today? The Bible has nothing to say about modern things like drugs, so how can it tell me what to do? We have heard all the Bible stories since we were small children, so why do we want to hear them again? How can we tell adults our doubts when they seem to have it all together? They do not know what our problems are.

4. Teens Teach Kids. Youth hand out a lump of clay the size of a Ping-Pong ball to each child. Ask children to close their eyes and think about God with you. Say to them: *What does God look like? Make God out of the clay in your hand.* Some possibilities include a rocking chair that comforts and enfolds us, a lamp that helps us see our way, or a huge rock that cannot be moved. Allow about ten minutes for this. Have each child tell the others in the group about what he or she has made and what it represents. Be sure to show them your image of God.

As children are making their images of God, talk among yourselves about how you are a model and a teacher for younger children. How can you share your faith with children? How would you handle their tough questions, such as: Why do bad things happen to people? or Why can't we see God?

5. Tell the Story Through Art. Draw a picture of a stained glass window on drawing paper. Depict an event or character from Jesus' ministry. The group may want to assign individuals a topic so that the whole life of Jesus is cov-

ered. The Good News Bible has simple drawings to give you ideas. Use permanent black marker for the outline and colored markers for the glass. Wipe the paper lightly with cooking oil and a paper towel. The picture will become translucent like a stained glass window. Use a black construction paper frame. Place these stained glass pictures on the windows sills when you return to the worship area.

6. Write Your Story. Participants will write stories that tell how they learned about faith and how God has been at work in their lives. Allow some time to read or tell the stories. Encourage writers to share their stories in the church newsletter or on a bulletin board, if they wish.

7. Tell Your Story. Youth and adults tell their stories of faith to each other. Invite participants to tell their earliest memory of God, who their first Sunday school teacher was, who influenced them most in their faith, and how they have influenced others.

8. Sing the Story. Sing the hymns and songs that tell the story of Jesus. Begin by learning the hymn "If All You Want, Lord" (Troeger/Doran) or other faith hymn, which you will sing during the offering. Then sing through the whole story of Jesus' life beginning with the nativity songs, songs about Jesus' ministry, passion songs, and resurrection hymns. End with "Jesus Loves Me." Give the children rhythm instruments and have a collection of songbooks and hymnals on hand.

Gathering Hymns

Have people gather again in the worship area and sit with other members of their faith center group. Sing as a congregation until everyone has returned. Suggested hymns include: "Two Fishermen" (Toolan), "Blessed Assurance" (Crosby/Knapp), "Lord of the Dance" (Carter).

Sharing Our Stories

(a time for the congregation to share joys, concerns, insights)

Pastoral Prayer

Offering

Worship Leader: The thing that we pass on to our children, perhaps earlier than anything else, is the way we handle and value money. Children sense that money has great importance, because families are always conserving it or trading it for things they want. As we offer our gifts of money today, let us be an example to the children, showing them that all our gifts belong to God. We are not so much offering up our portion as we are giving back what was God's to begin with.

Prayer of Dedication

Litany of Commitment and Faith

One: Hear, O children of God:

The Lord is our God, the Lord alone.

Group 1: We will love the Lord our God with all our heart, with all our soul, with all our might.

We will keep God's word in our heart.

Group 2: We will recite God's word to our children.

We will remind one another to study God's word.

Group 3: When our youth ask, we will tell them how God has walked with us on our journey. Like Lois and Eunice we will share our stories with them. We will kindle their faith with words of affirmation and love.

Group 4: We will remember that we are God's representatives. We have been made in God's image. We will be this image to children who look to us to see who God is.

Group 5: We are God's work of art. Like stained glass we will let God's love shine through us. We will let our lives tell the good news. Like a beautiful banner, we will let God use our lives to proclaim God's story.

Group 6: We will set aside time each day to be quiet before God and hear God speak.

Group 7: We will not hesitate to tell of the glorious deeds of the Lord. We will tell of the mighty wonders God has done.

Group 8: With hymns and songs we will praise the Lord our Maker, for God has done wondrous things.

All: We go forth knowing whose we are.

We go forth knowing we are loved by God.

We go forth to live the Story.

One: Go, children of God, go in peace.

Hymn of Commission

"Go, My Children" (Vajda/Welsh folk melody)

Benediction

Go now knowing that you are the people of God.

Go, remembering that you are a people with a history and a people with a future.

Go to live the story and to tell the story.

And may the blessing of God be with us all now and forevermore. Amen.

Yet Will I Rejoice and Give Thanks

Celebrate Thanksgiving

Though the fig tree does not blossom, and no fruit is on the vines; though the produce of the olive fails and the fields yield no food; . . . yet I will rejoice in the Lord; I will exult in the God of my salvation.

—Habakkuk 3:17-18

Thanksgiving is traditionally celebrated to give thanks for the abundant blessings in our lives. Harvest prayers around the world are uttered in thanks for the ample food, warm shelter, loving families, and political freedom.

This thanksgiving celebration, however, focuses not on abundance, but on the gratitude we feel even when things are scarce. We often think of abundance as a reward for our good behaviour or faith. We associate abundance with God's favour and the result of our virtues. But Christian thanksgiving is something altogether different. It is the recognition that God helps us even when we are not deserving. That is the nature of grace. We cannot do anything to deserve it. We can only reject it or accept it with gratitude.

In this celebration, we remember a period of history in which people struggled, made mistakes, and were not always very deserving. It was the early period of European emigration to the new world. In what was perhaps God's attempt to give the undeserving a little grace, the indigenous people living here helped the Europeans survive their first years in a harsh environment. Many of the forms of thanksgiving in this celebration are Native American prayers and

songs. They remind us that God loves us even when we are not very lovable, and for that we give thanks.

Bible Text

Acts 2; Luke 17:11-19; Psalm 65; Habakkuk 3

Biblical Background for Our Celebration

The early church is described in Luke 2 as a group of believers who were distinguished by their devotion to the teaching of the apostles, to their fellowship with each other, to the *breaking of bread,* and to *prayer.* The meaning of *breaking of bread* here has been debated. Some scholars say it refers to a type of Jewish fellowship meal called the *chaburah.* In this case it was a meal that demonstrated the believers' mutual love and recalled their association with Jesus. Some scholars think that it was an early commemoration of Christ's death. Still others think it was an agape feast that emphasized the joy of communion with the risen Lord and the fellowship with each other. Whatever it may have been, it does not seem to have any paschal significance in which the bread and cup are the very body and blood of Christ. However, since Luke places this passage between two important terms, *fellowship* and *prayer*, it sounds like it is part of the liturgy and not just a time to eat. In any case, all Jewish meals were an occasion for joy, love, and praise. This is what will be captured in this service. Although our everyday meals are occasions for thanksgiving, it is important to deliberately set aside special times to offer thanks for the gift of grace that we need, but do not deserve.

Luke 17:11-19, the story of Jesus healing ten lepers, is a perfect illustration of proper Christian gratitude. After Jesus heals the lepers of their dread disease, only one turns back to thank Jesus. The story demonstrates that God's grace is freely given. Grace does not require penance, indulgences, or even gratitude as a precondition. But the one who remembers to give thanks and to acknowledge the source of healing and grace is blessed by deep faith. It is notable that all ten lepers were healed. The one who expressed gratitude received no more than did the others. Those who did not express thanks did not lose what they had been given; there was no punishing miracle returning them to their leprous state.

Ingratitude is, perhaps, the most common of all human failings. Recognizing this, the psalms many times call us to thanksgiving. One such psalm is Psalm 65. This is a song of thanksgiving for the power and bounty of God. It reveals the proper spiritual sequence in one's approach to God: first, confession and forgiveness of sin; second, praise and supplication. The goodness (v. 4) enjoyed by those who had the privilege of worshiping God consisted of spiritual and temporal blessings. The worshipers received God's forgiveness and had fellowship and sharing of a meal (cf. Lev. 7:11-17).

Habakkuk, in his prayer, also invites us to thanksgiving. In his prayer the prophet remembers God's past faithfulness and the salvation stories from the creation and the Book of Exodus to the final revelation of God's rule and judgment. Rooted in the covenant is the prophet's confidence in the continuing presence of God. Special days, such as Thanksgiving, serve as a reminder to turn and thank God not out of duty or for assurance of future blessings, but because giving thanks is an impulse of faith and the awareness that we are worthy in our unworthiness.

Faith Nugget
Thanking God is an impulse of faith.

Early Preparation

1. Four weeks in advance select actors for the drama and plan rehearsals. Recruit musicians and the dance ensemble.

2. Give the music selection to the choir.

3. Meet with the worship leader and all leaders of the Thanksgiving centres and the worship leader and go through the service together. Select rooms for each learning centre. Remind each leader to plan and prepare for the group's presentation when the congregation reassembles.

4. Place a glass bowl or jar of dried corn at the front for the visual call to worship, and have all supplies in the rooms before the service begins.

You will need
☐ empty baskets, platters, and plates
☐ kernels of corn (five per person)
☐ slides to illustrate the hymn of praise
☐ copies of the drama
☐ Thanksgiving Celebration bulletins

Name of your church
Yet Will I Rejoice and Give Thanks
Celebrate Thanksgiving

Gathering

Call to Worship

Invocation

Hymn of Praise . . . . "Praise to God, Immortal Praise"

Prayer of Confession

Hymn . . . . "Praise Waits for Thee in Zion" (vv. 1-2)

Silent Confession

Assurance of Pardon

Scripture Reading

Message. . . . . "The Fig Tree Does Not Blossom"

Hymn of Response . . . . "Lord, Should Rising Whirlwinds"

Thanksgiving Centres

1. Break Bread Together. Meet in the kitchen to bake muffins to commemorate God's sufficient gifts.
2. Thanks to Native North Americans. Explore the gifts of Native North Americans, write a Bible verse in symbol, and pray an aboriginal prayer.
3. Games! Games! Games! Adults and children play table games that will help them think globally as they give thanks to God for the earth.
4. The Healing of the Ten Lepers. A Bible study of the story of the ten lepers.
5. Do a Service Project—to extend a little grace to others.
6. Tell Stories of Gratitude. Tell your faith story. Laugh and celebrate together.
7. Sing a Psalm. Musicians and aspiring composers compose music for Psalm 65.
8. Make a Thanksgiving Mosaic.
9. Take a Thanksgiving Walk. Explore outdoors, weather permitting.

Gathering Again

Offering

The Fellowship Meal

Pastoral Prayer

Hymn . . . . . . "When the Church of Jesus" "Worship the Lord" "The Church of Christ in Every Age"

Benediction

The Celebration

As you create the atmosphere for the celebration, emphasize scarcity instead of abundance. Help people express gratitude for God's grace without displaying all the usual symbols of abundance for Thanksgiving, such as the horn of plenty or great spreads of produce.

Gathering

Create a visual call to worship to focus attention on the theme as soon as people arrive. Place empty baskets, platters, or plates on a worship table. As people arrive, give them each five kernels of corn and ask them to sit down. In the bulletin suggest that for each kernel of corn they think of a way that God has been gracious to them, even when they did not deserve it. Just before the call to worship, invite people to bring their kernels of corn to the plates on the worship table, or pass the plates to collect the corn as a symbol of God's graciousness and our gratitude.

Call to Worship (based on Psalm 65)

> **One:** Praise is due to God in Zion
>
> **All:** who invites us to the house of God.
>
> **One:** Thanksgiving is due to God in Zion
>
> **All:** whose awesome deeds deliver us.
> Come, let us worship the God of our salvation.

Invocation

Creator God, our Deliverer, our Salvation, like the leper, we come for healing. Be with us, gracious Healer, and accept our worship. Like the disciples we come to share the good news and the bounty of the earth. Be with us, wise Provider, and accept our worship. Like the prophet Habakkuk, we will exult in you, O God

of our salvation. Accept, we pray, the offering of our worship and praise. Amen.

Hymn of Praise

"Praise to God, Immortal Praise" (Barbauld/Abbot) or a praise hymn of your choosing. This hymn may be sung by the choir or an ensemble while slides illustrating the hymn are shown.

Prayer of Confession

Hymn

"Praise Waits for Thee in Zion," verses 1-2 (Scottish Psalter/Smith), or a hymn of your choice

Silent Confession

Assurance of Pardon

[*The choir sings the following words to the tune of "Praise Waits for Thee in Zion"; then all sing verse 4 of this hymn.*]

> Hear the good news of love and grace,
> Forgiveness offered free
> Removing sin without a trace,
> Your soul restored shall be.

Scripture Reading

A reader reads Acts 2:44-47; Luke 17:11-19; Psalm 65:1-5; Habakkuk 3:17-19. Or chancel actors can dramatize one or more of the passages.

Message

"The Fig Tree Does Not Blossom"
A drama based on an actual event (see Resources for This Celebration)

Hymn of Response

"Lord, Should Rising Whirlwinds" (Barbauld/Corbeil) or response hymn of your choice

Worship Leader: The drama refers to some of the gifts given to our culture by the indigenous peoples of North America. Other gifts include worshipful music and dance by which we express our gratitude to God.

Have a dance ensemble learn an aboriginal circle dance performed to the hymn "Jesus A, Nahetotaetanome" ("Jesus Lord, How Joyful You Have Made Us") by John Heap of Birds, or "Ehane he'ame" ("Father God, You Are Holy") by Harvey Whiteshield. Both of these hymns are in *Hymnal: A Worship Book* and on the audio cassette tape *Hymnal Selections*, Vol. 1.

Here is a simple Native North American dance step: Tap left toe, drop left heel; tap right toe, drop right heel. Make up hand motions to illustrate the words to the hymn. You may wish to use a drum accompaniment.

Thanksgiving Centres

At the close of the dance, instruct celebrants to go to activity centres. As they leave encourage them to hum the last hymn and walk to the centres using the dance step. Inform them to sit together with their activity group when they return later.

1. Break Bread Together. This group will meet in the kitchen and make corn-meal muffins. Fill the muffin cups half full and add a little less than one teaspoon of jam. Cover with more batter and bake. About eight minutes before the close of time in the Thanksgiving centres, take muffins and a beverage, if you wish, to each group to use in their closing. Have each group leader begin the "meal" with: *In the passage that we heard from Acts 2, it says that the Christians gathered for "the breaking of bread."* Note: If your building allows, this fellowship meal may take place when all have gathered again in the auditorium.

2. Thanks to Native North Americans. Using information sheets found in the resource section, learn some of the many contributions that the native people have made to life and culture in North American society. Say a Native North American prayer to God, also in the resource section. Also try using the symbols in the resource section to write Psalm 65:1a.

3. Games! Games! Games! Write to Aga Khan Foundation Canada, Waterpark Place, 10 Bay Street, Suite 610, Toronto, Ontario, Canada M5J 2R8, to request your free copies of the SURVIVAL game, which is really a dozen games. You will receive permission to photocopy the game and the activity sheets. They include word searches, mazes, crosswords, and brainteasers. These games explore the issues of international development and care of the earth.

4. The Healing of the Ten Lepers. This activity is for age ten and up. The group will use various means to explore this Bible story. Have someone read Luke 17:11-19. Then give out the question sheet found in the resource section. If children need help, either read each part aloud or pair them with a reader. Tell the group that there are no right answers. The questions ask people to tell how they *feel*.

When everyone has finished the question sheet, the leader will lead a discussion about the responses. If there is time, do any or all of the following: draw a picture of the story of the lepers; sing some of the songs that came to mind when you answered No. 6; act out the story; imagine what happened next in the story; have a discussion about giving thanks, bringing up issues such as why we fail to celebrate the good fortune of others, why we forget to give thanks, and how we assume that we have a right to good health and good fortune.

5. Do a Service Project. The group leader will have a list of possible service projects, or the group may suggest others. Plan a project and make a commitment to carry it out. Begin with a discussion of service as a natural response to God's goodness to us. Some ideas for a project include service to retirement homes, drop-in centres, cancer patients who need rides to treatment and appointments, schools that need volunteers, highway department that needs volunteers to clean up highway areas, or hospitals that need volunteers. As a group decide on a project and the term of commitment. Let the congregation know of your project and keep them informed.

6. Tell Stories of Gratitude. Arrange ahead of time for several people to begin with their own faith stories of gratitude to God. Then encourage others in the group to tell their stories. Particularly encourage stories of the awareness of the presence of God in difficult times. Decide how the group will summarize their stories when the whole congregation regathers. Consider sharing a dialogue or story with the congregation.

7. Sing a Psalm. This group will put Psalm 65, a psalm that was originally sung, to a common tune or compose original music. Also, learn to sing a thanksgiving round, such as "From the Hands" (Janzen/Warkentin) or "Lord, Bless the Hands" (Murray/Murray). In advance ask people to bring musical instruments. Provide music manuscript paper and pencils and pitch pipe.

8. Make a Thanksgiving Mosaic. Each person outlines a design in pencil, depicting thanksgiving on a piece of poster board, thin wood, or masonite. Have containers of seeds of many colours and sizes. Seeds such as corn, sunflowers, split peas, and lentils are easy to work with and provide lots of colour. Spread glue in the portion of the picture to be covered by one type of seed. Pour on seeds, spreading them around and brushing off excess seeds onto paper. Return extra seeds to their containers. Fill in remaining portions of the design, one at a time, until the picture is finished. Display the artwork for the congregation to see.

9. Take a Thanksgiving Walk. If the weather is suitable, take a Polaroid camera outdoors to capture God's creation on film. If you have a naturalist in the group, ask her or him to point out those things that might otherwise be missed. Return indoors to write prayers or poems of thanksgiving based on the pictures. Display the photos with the prayers.

Gathering Again

As groups finish their activities, return to the sanctuary or gathering place for more congregational celebration. Encourage people to sit with their groups instead of returning to their families. Sing hymns of thanksgiving until everyone has returned to the worship area.

When everyone has gathered again, the worship leader invites groups to share something from their activity, calling on one group at a time. He or she says:

> Come, ye thankful people, come. Come, Group 2, and show us the gifts we have received from the Native peoples.
>
> Come, Group 2, Group 4, Group 8, and Group 9, and show us your work of art. [*Group 8 displays its mural, Groups 4 and 9 put up their art work, and Group 2 puts up its symbols for Psalm 65.*]
>
> Come, someone from Group 6, and tell us a story of thanksgiving.
>
> Come, Group 7, and sing us a Psalm.
>
> Come, Group 5, and tell us about your service project.

Offering

> **Worship Leader:** People in the world who have little often seem the most generous. Like the widow who gave the mite, they will go to great lengths to share what little they have with the stranger, the orphan, and the poor. If times are as lean as we always say they are during the annual stewardship drive, let us give all the more generously.

If your facilities allow, everyone can bring their offering forward. Otherwise, the ushers will receive the offering as a hymn is sung. Choose from hymns such as "What Gift Can We Bring" (Marshall) or "As Saints of Old" (von Christierson/Sateren).

As ushers bring the offering forward, have Group 7 sing the round they learned or the song they composed.

The Fellowship Meal

Worship Leader: Come, Group 1, and serve us our fellowship meal. Every meal is a sacred time of thanksgiving and praise. [*Here the muffins will be served after a grace is sung unless you have done this in the group setting.*] The cornmeal reminds us of the five kernels of corn and the difficult times we may face. The surprise inside is there to remind us that in the midst of difficult times, God is there walking with us.

Pastoral Prayer

O God, it is easy to give thanks in good times. But in bad times, we also have every reason to give thanks to you, our Protector, Sustainer, and Saviour. Historians tell us that the Pilgrims had the custom of putting five kernels of corn on each empty plate before the Thanksgiving dinner was served. They remembered to be grateful even when food was scarce. Our worship is about you, after all, not about our accomplishments, trials, and wishes. Send us from this place with deep gratitude for you and all that you have done for the people of God.

Hymn

Sing a hymn of commission, such as "When the Church of Jesus" (Green/Smith) or "Worship the Lord" (Kaan) or "The Church of Christ in Every Age" (Green/Bristol).

Benediction

[*please stand if you are able*]

Centre 2.

Contributions of Native North Americans

Often European Americans are unaware how much they owe to native peoples who helped the first European immigrants survive their first years in the New World. Did you know that American Indian nations introduced the following to our culture?

1. Many foods and plants —turkeys, corn, sweet potatoes, potatoes, tomatoes, bell and chili peppers, pimentos, lima beans, pole beans, navy beans, kidney beans, squash, pumpkins, avocados, peanuts, pecans, cashews, guava, pineapples, cassava root, vanilla, sunflowers, petunias, black-eyed susans, dahlias, marigolds, zinnias, poinsettias.

When the Spanish arrived in Peru a few years after Columbus's landfall, the Indians of the Andes had been growing potatoes for 4,000 years and they had 3,000 varieties. (Today there are only 250 varieties left.) The conquistadors, who were looking for gold were not impressed, but they took potatoes back to Europe. Proving to be ideal for the northern European soil and climate, this vegetable saved the Irish from starvation after Oliver Cromwell's Roundheads pushed the people of Ireland into the barren province of Connacht. The potato became the dominant food of northern Europe's working class.

2. Medicines. The New World had been malaria-free until mosquitoes tasted infected Europeans. But the native found a cure in the seventeenth century, deriving quinine from the bark of the cinchona tree, which grew on the slopes of the Peruvian Andes. It was quinine that enabled the Europeans to colonize the tropics. Indigenous people also gave the world willow bark, which contains salicin, the drug now used in synthetic form in aspirin. Banting's work (insulin) was based on native medicine, as were birthing techniques, birth control, and teas to cure and prevent scurvy.

3. Names. We use many names that come from the languages of indigenous groups. *Alabama* means "clearers of the thicket"; *Alaska*, "great land"; *Arizona*, "place of little springs." Other place names include: *Arkansas, Connecticut, Idaho, Illinois, Iowa, Kansas, Kentucky, Massachusetts, Michigan, Minnesota, Mississippi, Missouri, Nebraska, New Mexico, Dakota, Ohio, Oklahoma, Ottawa, Ohio, Tennessee, Texas, Utah, Wisconsin, Wyoming.* A few words in common use today include *canoe, hammock, poncho, cocoa.*

4. Ecology. Many Native North American groups hold great reverence for all creation. The centrality of God's creation in Native North American religion can be compared with the Old Testament idea of creation as one united, interconnected household created and loved by God.

5. Games. Just about anything that bounces originated with Native Americans, such as basketball and hockey.

6. Government. The Constitution of the United States of America borrows heavily from democratic practices of the Iroquois.

7. Symbols. Many of the common symbols in use today are taken from rock paintings of the indigenous peoples.

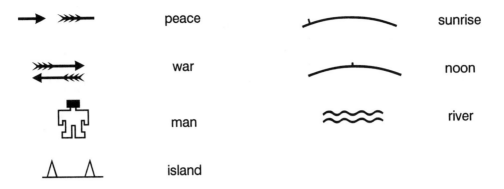

→ ≫≫	peace
≫≫ → ← ≪≪	war
(figure)	man
Λ Λ	island

(arc)	sunrise
(arc)	noon
∿∿∿	river

The Circle Prayer

Native North Americans have a rich religious tradition of spirituality and prayer. The prayer below symbolizes faith as a circle and fellowship as the four earthly directions. Stand in a circle and pray this prayer together.

One: We are gathered in a circle aware that there is a centre to our circle of life. We will move to face each of the four sacred directions by turning clockwise as each direction is named.

Let us pray:
We give thanks for this time together to honour the Creator God. May we be as faithful in worship as our elder brother the sun is in caring for us this day, and as grandmother moon is in watching over the nights of our lives.

We give thanks for the gifts of each of the directions and acknowledge that it is the Creator's intention that all nations would come together from the four directions. Let us face south and remember that it is the home of people of black skin. It is the direction we look when we seek the warmth of the sun.

All: May we recognize the promise of rebirth among all living things in this part of our Mother the Earth, as we await the warm winds of the south.

One: Let us turn to the west, which reminds us of the people of red skin and is the direction that teaches about the need for rest.

All: May the setting sun find us at peace with each other so that we will have no fear of the darkness.

One: Let us turn to the north, which is the direction of people of white skin and is the direction of coolness and clarity of thought.

All: May the winter winds give us clear vision of how all life can be nurtured and sustained.

One: Let us turn to the east, which reminds us of the people of yellow skin and is the direction of first light.

All: May the light of each dawn enable us to see with new clarity the beauty of creation and give thanks to the Creator that we have a place in each new day. Amen.

Centre 4.

If I Had Been There

1. If I had been in Galilee and had seen Jesus heal the ten lepers, I would have felt . . . (*check those that apply*)

- ☐ **disbelief**—they could not have been healed like that!
- ☐ **annoyed** with the ones who did not say thank you.
- ☐ **excited** and happy to see these people made well.
- ☐ **envious** that nothing like this ever happened to me.
- ☐ **embarrassed** that the only one who gave thanks was a foreigner.
- ☐ **reminded** of the times I did not say thank you.
- ☐ **other**:

If you checked more than one, underline the one about which you felt the strongest.

2. For me, the main point of this story is

3. I identify most with (*check one*)

- ☐ **the leper** calling out for healing.
- ☐ **the nine** who went on their way.
- ☐ **the one** who turned back to say thanks.
- ☐ **Jesus** who did the healing.

4. If I had to describe the ten lepers with a colour it would be

5. If I had to describe with a colour how the lepers felt after they were healed, it would be

6. If the lepers sang a song, what song might they have sung? (*Name a popular song or hymn.*) Would the one who returned have a different song? If so, what might it have been?

7. Share a story about a time when you felt something like that leper who turned back.

The Fig Tree Does Not Blossom

Production Notes: No costumes or stage settings are needed. The congregation can supply these with their imagination. If the actors are unable to memorize their lines, they should be well rehearsed and read without allowing the scripts to be the obvious focal points. The title is from Habakkuk 3:17. The event regarding the five kernels is true. The dialogue and the names are fictitious.

Setting: It is a cold February day in the Boston Bay area, eleven years after the Pilgrims arrived at Plymouth. The year is 1631. The scene opens with a gathering of colonists. A meeting has been called at the home of one of the leaders of the colony.

Cast: Thomas Muldon—a man in his forties, a leader in the colony
Jenny Muldon—wife of Thomas
Melinda Taft—a woman in her thirties
Dorlean Hood—a woman in her forties
George Fenwick—a man of fifty
Corbett Spivey—a man in his twenties. He is angry and in despair.
Foster Cobb—a single man in his twenties

Thomas: Thank you for coming out. We had hoped that there would be more here for such an important meeting.

Melinda: Who would have thought that we would have such terrible weather in February. I am sure that the Blakes can not possibly get through the snow at their place.

George: I don't think that anyone from over by the Crow's Foot can possibly get here either. It's not just the snow, it's the driving wind.

Jenny: And Mrs. Firth still has not recovered from childbirth. She shouldn't be left alone so that means Mr. Firth will not be here. I think we'd better begin. There won't be any more coming now.

Thomas: I guess you know why we are meeting.

Dorlean: I hope it is to give us good news of the *Lyon*. How many months is it now since we sent that ship back to England to get supplies?

George: [*mentally counting the months*] ...July...um...

George and Dorlean: [*their words overlap*] Eight months...

George: Should have been back long before this.

Corbett: Let's cut the chitchat and get on with it. I suppose you have bad news. Let's get it over with. Is there anything other than bad news in this stinking rotten place? Another crop failure. We haven't eaten a decent meal in months. Our cellar is empty. I have not been able to find even one squirrel this week. It's those stinking Indians that have killed off all the wild animals and left us with nothing. I'd even settle for a lousy rat and I can't even find one of those. The kid's crying—he's hungry. The wife is sick. The way I see it, we're all going to starve in this godforsaken place. Out with your bad news! I've had it. Maybe we should get our guns and give those Indians a little visit and liberate some of all that meat they must have stashed away!

Foster: Yeah. I think I could find some gunshot for that, Corb.

Jenny: I'm sorry your wife is sick, Mr. Spivey. Most of us are just about down to our last potato too. But I must object to your remarks about our Indian neighbours.

Foster: Neighbours! Listen to the woman!

Jenny: Those of us who came eleven years ago know that we owe our lives to these Indians. We would never have made it through even that first year if they had not shown us how to survive. They gave us beans and pemmican. They taught us how to make pemmican.

Foster: [*interrupting*] Stuff it. Those savages . . .

Dorlean: Mr. Cobb! You were not here eleven years ago. Mrs. Muldon is right. We would not have survived without the help of the Indians. You have no idea what it was like that first winter. They loaned us toboggans—we had no experience with all this snow. They showed us how to make shelters.

Thomas: She's right, you know. We take it all for granted now. But we learned from them to make canoes. We would have starved without their potatoes and corn and . . .

Jenny: And maybe died without their medicines.

Foster: What's any of this got to do with what we're here for?

Corbett: The cold weather has addled these women's heads. We owe nothing to our red [*sarcastically*] neighbours! Poachers!

George: I did not want to bring this up, Mr. Spivey, but I cannot stand by and let you malign the ladies. You know that the Indians showed us never to kill a doe, especially one with unborn young. And always to keep enough seed for the coming planting. I have seen you bring down a doe *and her young!*

Corbett: [*begins to protest*] I . . . I . . .

Thomas: It's true, Mr. Spivey. I too saw you. And on more than one occasion. And not just deer. And you know that you have taken too many young animals.

Melinda: And wasted what you didn't want at the time.

Corbett: What is this! Gang up on Corbett Spivey time? I know you have it in for me. All of you. Just because I am a better hunter than any of you.

[*He jumps up.*]

Stick with your stinking Indians. I'm leaving! I can use a gun on more than deer, you know!

Thomas: [*gets up to block his way*]

Sit down, Corbett. We're all in this together.

[*Corbett stops but does not sit down. Thomas remains standing with him.*]

Dorlean: Sit down with us, Mr. Spivey. We're all feeling short-tempered. We're all hungry. And cold. And we all could confess to being care-less—of wasting—of not saving enough seed and killing animals too young. I know we thought the ship would be here by now, and we ate our seed potatoes and [*she hesitates, trying to keep back the tears*] we have eaten all of our corn—even our seed corn. We just could not help it. The children were crying for something to eat . . . [*her voice trails off*]

George: If this is confession time, I guess most of us could confess.

[*He puts his head in his hands.*]

I know I have things to confess. I guess most of us have contrib-uted to our scarcity of food.

[*The room becomes quiet.*]

Foster: It feels like a blinkin' Quaker meeting in here. Let's get on with it.

Corbett: [*obviously uncomfortable*]

Yeah. Like I said. Give us the bad news, Thomas, and get it over with. I'm going.

Thomas: [*standing centre stage*]

As you have suspected, we have had no word from England. We do not know if the *Lyon* even reached England much less if it is on its way back. To put it bluntly our situation is desperate. As you know, the snow has covered the acorns, and even if there were any left we have been unable to dig them out. The storms have prevented us from getting any mussels.

Corbett: Cut the litany, Thomas. We all know all that.

[*He gets up to leave again. Foster gets him to sit down and Thomas continues.*]

Thomas: The common storehouse of grain has been used to the limit be-cause of the crop failure. We gave out more than we should have because we too counted on the *Lyon* being here. We didn't expect all these immigrants who came so unprepared and with no food supplies.

Corbett: [*angrily*] I said, get on with it, Thomas! We know all that stuff.

Thomas: Today the leaders checked to see exactly how much we have left. We have calculated that from now on each person will receive [*pause*] five kernels of corn per day.

[*There is an audible gasp.*]

Dorlean: You mean five cobs?

Thomas: No. I'm sorry. Five kernels.

[*He opens a sack and holds out five kernels.*]

Five kernels.

Here, Mrs. Hood.

[*He places five kernels on her hand. In stunned silence she stares at the five kernels.*]

Here, Corbett.

[*He holds out the five kernels.*]

Corbett: [*He slaps Thomas's hand from the bottom, scattering the corn.*]

And just how many hours will that keep me alive? And how is my kid supposed to chew that? Keep your miserable corn and let us die today instead of tomorrow.

[*When the corn goes flying, Melinda goes about trying to find it and pick it up.*]

Foster: Five kernels! We may as well have nothing. I'm with Corbett. Keep your paltry corn.

Melinda: Here is your corn, Mr. Spivey. I have some corn I can share.

Corbett: You have some corn! Hoarder! So you're one of those, are you?

Melinda: [*ignoring his outburst, continues*]

My husband and I did as the leaders advised us. We used one-tenth of our crops as our tithe, one-tenth we saved for seed corn, one-tenth we saved for a time of emergency, and the rest we used for our daily needs. I would like to give our saved corn to the nurses and let them decide how it should be distributed.

George: [*looking at five kernels on his hand*]

Five kernels a day.

Jenny: I'm sorry, Mr. Fenwick. I know your family needs more. Everyone does. I guess we're all asking how God could let this happen to us.

Foster: Corbett was right. It is a godforsaken place.

George: Actually I was thinking just the opposite. I was thinking we should be giving thanks.

Dorlean and
Corbett: Giving thanks?

Corbett: What on earth for?

George: For people who are willing to share—like Mrs. Taft who saved corn as we were told to do. Maybe there are others who have some too. And for the bounty that the earth can provide—if we co-operate with nature. And, I guess, for the fact that we have survived these eleven years.

Jenny: You are right, George. I guess all of us have been feeling bitter. You have made me do some thinking. It's easy to blame God. It's hard to give thanks.

Thomas: Perhaps we can do just that now. Let's stand and offer a prayer of thanks for what we *do* have.

Jenny: [*reaches for Dorlean and they stand together*]

It's warmer when we huddle anyway!

[*She puts her arm around Dorlean.*]

[*Corbett moves away from the "circle" that is forming and moves toward the door. However, as Thomas begins to pray, he moves in and reaches a hand to Thomas's shoulder.*]

Thomas: Loving God, we are cold and hungry and discouraged, yet we give you thanks . . .

[*The group freezes to end the drama.*]

Narrator: These settlers did survive. Not many days after this time of offering thanks to God for what they did have, the ship *Lyon* returned with medicine, food, and other supplies.

We Await the Christ Who Liberates

Celebrate Advent

All praise to you eternal Son
Whose Advent has our freedom won.

—Charles Coffin

And would we others see God's face
Then justice must our lives embrace.

—Source unknown

The time of Advent puts us in an ironic situation. We are invited to look forward with great expectation to a tremendous event, an event that is the beginning point of a drama that unfolds as the Christian story. And yet, at the same time, we know that this event has already occurred. In order to look forward with anticipation, we need to enter into the scriptural mind-set of "the already but not yet." We see the promises of God as all at once fulfilled and being fulfilled and yet to be fulfilled. When we look at the scriptures and read them as if for the first time, then again under the leadership of the Holy Spirit, we will hear the old new message of God's purpose and plan for the church and for the world. Some of it has come to pass, but much of it is yet to be. Each Advent, we wait on the verge of a stupendous happening, a happening that invites our participation in its unfolding.

Bible Text

Luke 1:1-56; Luke 4:16-21

Bible Background for Our Celebration

Mary's well-known hymn in Luke 1:46-56 is called the Magnificat. It is much more than an individual hymn of praise and thanksgiving for personal blessing received. This hymn offers praise for God's mindfulness of and love for the poor and the oppressed. It pictures Israel as the servant of God who needs help and needs to be helpful. It sees that the promises God gave long ago to Abraham are now being accomplished.

Just before the Magnificat, Luke tells how John and Jesus come together while they are still in their mothers' wombs. It is a scene that reminds us of Esau and Jacob in the womb of Rebecca (Gen. 25). In the Old Testament story, there is a struggle between the brothers for birthrights and privileges before the children are ever born. In contrast, when John and Jesus come together, there is great joy. John leaps for joy. A new age of reconciliation has been heralded. Just as Mary is a player in this drama of God Incarnate, so too will the people of God be participants in the fulfillment of God's promises to fill the hungry with good things and raise up the lowly. Mary's hymn of praise is a forerunner of the prophecy proclaimed by Jesus when he read Isaiah 61 and announced release to the captives and liberation for the oppressed. These passages set the entire scene for the life and ministry of Jesus and redramatize the ancient promises of God that are before us.

Faith Nugget

At Advent we celebrate what has already been accomplished and joyfully anticipate what is yet to be fulfilled.

Early Preparation

1. Planners and leaders meet six to eight weeks in advance. All should read the material for this service. Buy or borrow the book *Unexpected Good News by Robert McAfee Brown*, and share it with the leaders.

2. Purchase the banner materials and the symbols material.

3. Select a location for each Advent centre.

4. Find readers for the message, "Can We Sing the Song of Mary?" Give them the material for their rehearsal. They may use a script but they should read as though they are telling their own story. Similarly, recruit readers for the four Sundays of Advent.

5. Cut the small chain strips to be given to each person who enters to worship, and make the large chain that will be placed on the table at the front.

6. Find a large white birch branch or paint a large branch of any deciduous tree with white paint. This tree will take the place of the usual evergreen Christmas tree. leftover white house paint will work.

7. Collect food for food hampers. Get boxes.

8. Have Advent centre leaders gather materials and get project information from agencies. Get addresses for letter writing project.

9. Ask soloist to prepare "The Magnificat."

10. See the Top Secret section in the Resources for This Celebration. Ask a bugle band with tambourines to rehearse the music and the choric reading. Have the choir learn the hymn "On Jordan's Banks the Baptist's Cry." Note: This is an opportunity to remind worship leaders and musicians that during Advent, Advent hymns, NOT Christmas hymns, should be sung.)

You will need

- ☐ materials for banners and symbols
- ☐ readers
- ☐ materials for the large chain/arcs of the rainbow
- ☐ strips of paper and glue or tape for small chains
- ☐ soloist
- ☐ bugle band with tambourines
- ☐ bulletins
- ☐ large white branch in a tree stand or bucket of sand
- ☐ banner standard

Your church name

We Await the Christ Who Liberates
Celebrate Advent

Gathering

Call to Worship

Hymn of Praise . . . . "Blessed Be the God of Israel"

Advent Ceremony

Prayer of Confession

Silent Reflection (Procession of Chains)

Assurance of Pardon

The Advent Story

Hymn . . . . "Woman in the Night"

Scripture. . . . . Luke 1:46-56
Luke 4:16-21

Solo . . . . "The Magnificat"

Message. . . . . "Can We Sing the Song of Mary?"

Procession to Advent Centres

Advent Centres

1. Decorate the Church. Children and adults make ornaments.
2. Prepare and Wait. Children and adults talk about waiting for the promise while they make creches.
3. Do Something About It. Respond to the morning message.
4. Encourage Disciples. Write letters to encourage people involved in liberating ministries.
5. Pack Food Boxes. Talk about the message while packing food boxes for a local food pantry.
6. Study the Bible. Look at the four Bible characters featured in the Advent ceremonies.
7. Who Needs It? Identify people in your community who need the liberating ministry of Christ.
8. Jesus, Economics, and Politics. Tackle the difficult political issues in Mary's song.

Gathering Hymn. . . . . "Hail to the Lord's Anointed"

Offering

Pastoral Prayer

Hymn: . . . . "On Jordan's Banks the Baptist's Cry"

Benediction

The Celebration

Advent celebrates the fulfilment of God's promise to dwell among us and anticipates the fulfilment of the promise of liberation—liberation from sin and guilt, but also liberation from poverty, oppression, and powerlessness. Incarnation has been accomplished. Liberation is yet to be fully achieved.

Thus, we anticipate the thing that is to come. This Advent celebration focuses on the coming of our liberator, Jesus, and the hope for our liberation. These are not typical Christmas or Advent themes, but when we read Mary's song of praise, we see that the true meaning of Christ's coming is to fulfill God's promise to send a liberator to feed the hungry, free the captives, and empower the powerless. At the beginning of his ministry (see Luke 4), Jesus reiterates this reason for his coming. Advent is the time to renew our commitment as people of faith to help God's liberation happen.

Plan a visual call to worship that people will notice as they enter the worship place. To one side at the front, anchor a large, bare, white branch in a Christmas tree stand or bucket of sand. Hang a large plain banner of blue felt or velveteen on a wall or standard near the centre of the worship area. On a worship table place a large chain, made from the shapes that will eventually adorn the banner (see banner instructions in the resource section). Be prepared to use the banner and chain for the whole season of Advent and Christmas.

As people arrive, hand them a strip of construction paper that will later become a link in a paper chain symbolizing our captivity and liberation.

Call to Worship

Worship Leader: Come, let us magnify the Lord and rejoice in God our Saviour.

God looks on us with favour and compassion.

God has shown mercy from generation to generation.

Come, let us magnify the Lord together.

Come let us worship God.

Hymn of Praise

"Blessed Be the God of Israel" (Perry/Webb)

The Advent Ceremony

On the first Sunday of Advent, begin an Advent ritual of liberation that will continue through all weeks of the season. The first ritual is provided here. See the resource section for ceremonies for the following weeks and Christmas.

Worship Leader: When you entered, each of you was given a slip of paper. Following the prayer of confession and during the silent reflection, all of you who care to are invited to bring your paper to the tree and help create a paper chain to adorn it. The chain will represent whatever it is in your life that needs to be unchained. You may be a slave to stereotypes based on race, sex, creed, or money. You may be burdened by a need to control others. You may be captive to a constant desire for material things. You may lack compassion for the disadvantaged both here and in other countries. You may be weighted down by old wrongs. Whatever your oppression, only you and God know.

Prayer of Confession(*in unison*)

Gracious God, we confess that sometimes we do not want to give you praise when we see the lowly raised up and the hungry filled with good things. We confess the times that we have not rejoiced when the slave, the oppressed, the addict, the unemployed have been set free. We confess the times when we have not participated in your liberating acts in the world. Remove the scales that blind us so that we may know our sin. By your mercy heal us so that justice may roll down like waters, and righteousness like an ever-flowing stream. Amen.

Silent Reflection

Procession of Chains

As people add their link to the chain, the choir softly sings "Set My Spirit Free" or other hymn of liberation.

Assurance of Pardon

Worship Leader: Hear the good news! The Mighty One has done great things. God's mercy is for all who will accept. God is faithful and just to forgive us our sins. You are the forgiven people of God.

The worship leader or other designated person goes to the tree and removes several links of chain and drops them into a waste container. He or she puts the manger and the hay on the banner.

Week 1

Storyteller: [*A storyteller goes to the worship table and removes the red link from the chain.*] Today is the first Sunday of Advent. It is a time of waiting, active waiting. Not waiting-with-folded-hands waiting but waiting-with-open-ears-and-hearts-and- commitment-to-carry-out-what-God-calls-us-to-do waiting. Mary said that God would bring to the world justice and righteousness and thanksgiving and compassion. Each week we will have stories of God at work. [*Pause slightly before beginning the story of Onesimus.*]

Hymn

"Woman in the Night" (Wren/Hamm) or any hymn based on the Magnificat

Scripture

Luke 1:46-56; Luke 4:16-21

Solo

"The Magnificat"

Message

"Can We Sing the Song of Mary?" (see Resources for This Celebration—performed by a readers theatre group, seven people scattered in the congregation)

Hymn

"Hail to the Lord's Anointed" (Montgomery/Farmer)

After the singing of this hymn, the pianist plays while the people move to the Advent centres.

Advent Centres

1. Decorate the Church. God gave the rainbow as a sign of covenant with Noah and all humanity, all creatures never again to destroy the earth. You may think that it is unusual to use this symbol at Christmas time. To do so with the familiar manger scene has two purposes. It reminds us how far God was willing to go to fulfill the promise, and it reminds us that the promise is to all peoples, not just to a chosen few. The rainbow with the manger is a powerful symbol of God's faithfulness and love for the world. As you work on the craft, reflect on the celebration message. Share your thoughts on other symbols that are meaningful.

This group will make manger and rainbow ornaments for the tree in the worship area. These will be made of cardboard. Trace the pattern in the resource section onto white poster board and cut out. Decorate with markers and glitter. Use a paper punch to make a hole at the top of the rainbow. Hang with a wire Christmas tree hanger or thread.

2. Prepare and Wait. Children and adults talk about waiting for the promise while they make creches. Begin by talking about ways to wait. If responses are slow, suggest such things as helping to bake, wrapping presents, shopping, cleaning the house, making decorations.

Waiting involves "doing" to make Christmas happen.

Using brightly coloured modelling clay that can be baked, each family makes figures for a small creche and stables from small boxes. Allow fifteen to twenty minutes for baking. While waiting for figures to bake, decorate the stable box. To close, ask if the activity helped to pass the time and think of Jesus at the same time. Pray together for patience to wait and awareness to see what God is doing in our world to fulfill the promise.

3. Do Something About It. Divide into pairs. One partner will be an oppressor. The other partner in each pair will be the oppressed. The oppressors may have the oppressed do whatever they order: (e.g., Roll a clothespin with your nose. Clean my glasses. Bow down and polish my shoes. Shout slogans.) It's the rule that the oppressed must obey. After five minutes, exchange roles. Now discuss the experience. How did you feel about being oppressed? about being the oppressor? Take about twenty minutes for this.

Now have the leader be the oppressor of the whole group. Make people do humiliating things to each other—within reason. Discuss. Did any of you refuse to obey? Did any band together to disobey together? Did the experience make you feel kinder or meaner? What does the Bible say about what our responses should be? Could you feel gratitude in your oppression as Mary did? For what was Mary thankful?

4. Encourage Disciples. In light of the message, identify people you know who are doing justice work. The leader should have compiled a list in case the group is unfamiliar with any such person. The list can include people in the congregation, such as social workers, chaplains, family lawyers, conflict mediators; denominational leaders, such as missionaries, voluntary service workers; community members, such as civic leaders who demand just laws; or world figures, such as Mother Teresa or people who work for Amnesty International.

Look at the work of some of these you have listed. Write letters of affirmation and encouragement. Ask those interested to take on a commitment of regular letter writing for Amnesty International and/or letters of encouragement to your missionaries.

5. Pack Food Boxes. Discuss the readers theatre, "Can We Sing the Song of

The Story of Onesimus

It was there is a cold dark prison in Rome that Paul met him. His name meant "useful" and how useful he proved to be! He was young and strong and just about to be set free. He was a great help to Paul. He saw something in Paul that he wanted. He wanted to become a Christian and Paul helped him on that journey. Onesimus was a slave who wanted to be free. It was his longing for freedom that got him into prison. What irony! It was in prison that he learned about Jesus, and now he had a new kind of freedom of which he had not even dreamed.

Philemon had been his owner. How unjust! How could this Christian man own another person? Unjust! Onesimus was shocked when Paul asked him to return to Colossae and go back to Philemon. But he trusted Paul and Paul had promised to send a letter with him to Philemon. In the letter Paul wrote that Onesimus was now Paul's brother in Christ. He wrote that Onesimus was like a son to Paul. He spoke of how followers of Christ are sisters and brothers—one family of God. He even suggested that Philemon consider Onesimus as

his brother. What a change! No longer a slave but a brother. We are not positive but it is believed that the Bishop of Ephesus, Bishop Onesimus, was this same Onesimus who had once been a slave. God opened the chain of injustice and replaced it with the rainbow arc of Christian community.

[*While this last part of the story is being told, two people open the chain and turn it to reveal the first arc of the rainbow—red. They carry the arc to the banner and place it on the banner. When the first arc of the rainbow is in place the storyteller continues.*]

The rainbow is a symbol of God's love for all people. It is a symbol of God's promise for all of creation. "For God so loved the world . . . ." We await the coming of Christ who will open the chain of injustice and make us one family of God.

[*As the links are removed each week and become the rainbow, the choir sings "O Healing River" or another hymn of reconciliation and healing*]

Mary?" Talk about peacemaking through justice. Have boxes and food items ready to pack for local distribution through a food bank. Discuss the politics of Mary's song as you pack. Appoint someone to deliver the boxes after the celebration.

6. Study the Bible. Study the Bible characters whose stories will be told in the Advent ceremony each Sunday of Advent. After summarizing each story, ask the group to look at the story in the Bible.

a. Onesimus and Philemon: Who needs liberation today? Would Paul's tactic work today? How would you go about liberating someone diplomatically today?

b. Vashti (Esther 1, 2): What modern parallels can you draw? Who are the Vashtis of today that you know? How can you help to free such people—both the powerful and the powerless?

c. Zacchaeus: Jesus said, "This day has salvation come to your house." Does our salvation and gratitude hit us in the pocketbook today? Should it? Someone has said that we can see the level of our Christianity by looking at our checkbook entries. Another has said, "Don't ask what a person believes, look at the [financial] decisions he makes." Discuss this statement.

7. Who Needs It? Identify people in your community who need the liberating ministry of Christ. Each of the characters in the readers theatre is based on a real situation. Think of similar people in the news now. Talk about the message in the reading, and think of examples from the news today. Prepare possible projects that the group could work on to minister to these people, and try to commit yourselves to carrying out some ministry. For example, provide assistance for a group home for youth or assist a shelter for battered women. Visit prisoners. Sponsor a missionary.

8. Jesus, Economics, and Politics. Tackle the difficult political issues in Mary's song. Appoint a leader to read

Robert McAfee Brown's *Unexpected Good News* (Westminster Press, 1984). Use chapter five, "Mary's Song: Whom Do We Hear?" as the basis of a discussion. Have several people read the dialogue recorded in this chapter. Then discuss it as a group. Using the earlier part of the chapter, talk about the political implications of Mary's song. Close by talking about how each one can commit himself or herself to acting on what they have learned.

Gathering Hymn

"Hail to the Lord's Anointed" (James Montgomery/John Farmer)

Offering

Worship leader: Church budgeting is a good symbol of Advent. It tells us what already is and what is not yet. We know the needs of the church program and we try to anticipate an inflow of funds. Let us live in the "not yet," giving as if the kingdom is upon us.

Pastoral Prayer

Hymn

"On Jordan's Banks the Baptist's Cry" (Coffin)

Top Secret Surprise

As few people as possible should be informed about this part of the service which will take place following the Pastoral Prayer. Unannounced, a bugle band bursts in playing the hymn "On Jordan's Bank the Baptist's Cry" or a bright fanfare for brass. Decorate bugles and tambourines with ribbons the colours of the rainbow. When the ensemble is assembled, members read the choral reading found on page 39 (based on Luke 3; Isaiah 52; 54; and Psalm 96).

Benediction

The band remains in place for the benediction, then marches out continuing to play as they recess. The people follow.

Banner Instructions

The banner may be used for all Sundays of Advent and Christmas worship, with new elements added each week. Several weeks ahead of the celebration, use the pattern here to make the banner and the applique pieces that will be added using Velcro. This way, the background may be used again at Easter. To enlarge these pattern pieces, project them on the wall using an overhead projector. When you have them projected to the size you want for the banner, trace them on newsprint.

Color key: hay—yellow; manger—brown; head of Christ—purple; bottom arc—red; second arc—yellow; third arc—green; fourth arc—indigo. Apply glitter or sequins to make the rainbow reflect light. When the banner is finished it will look like this.

The banner is made so that each coloured stripe in the rainbow can be removed separately and looped to form links in the chain that will be displayed on the worship table. To form the links in the chain, the coloured fabric arches must be stiffened with heavy iron-on facing or flexible cardboard. Use Velcro tabs on the chain side to attach the arc to the banner. Also use Velcro to close the loops in making the chain.

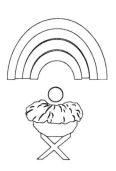

The circle that represents the Christ child is added for Christmas.

"Can We Sing the Song of Mary?"

Mary: My soul magnifies the Lord, and my spirit rejoices in God my Saviour. God is just and calls us to be a community of love.

Manuel: My name is Manuel. I live in the hills of Mexico. I am an Indian. My family of six lives in a one-room house. The roof is thatched. We can see between the poles that make up the walls. We are more fortunate than many of our neighbours, for once in two months we have some chicken to eat. Most of us here never have any kind of meat to eat. If we complain about our lot we are seen by the government as subversive. We have been shot at by the government soldiers. We have no health care. We have no schools for our children.

We are waiting. We are waiting for the Anointed One.

Manuel, Rita, Tom, Jane: We are waiting. We are waiting for the Anointed One.

We are waiting for good news for the poor.

We are waiting for release for the captives.

We are waiting for the oppressed to be set free.

Mary: My soul magnifies the Lord, and my spirit rejoices in God my Saviour. The Mighty One has done great things. God has brought freedom to the oppressed and filled the hungry with good things.

Rita: I am Rita. I live in the Philippines. My family and I had a small parcel of land where we grew our own food. Today the bulldozers came. Where we lived will become a shopping mall. I used to make baskets. Other artisans and I sold our work at a little co-op. Yesterday when I went to our market place the little shop was gone. The bulldozers had cleared it away.

Now we live under a bridge. We have been forced to become beggars. Does God hear our cry?

Will God look with pity on us, the dispossessed, the powerless?

We are waiting. We are waiting for the Anointed One.

Manuel, Rita, Tom, Jane: We are waiting. We are waiting for the Anointed One.

We are waiting for good news for the poor.

We are waiting for release for the captives.

We are waiting for the oppressed to be set free.

Mary: My soul magnifies the Lord and my spirit rejoices in God my Saviour.

God's mercy is for those who fear God from generation to generation.

God has brought down the powerful and lifted up the lowly.

Tom: I am Tom. I am a street kid. I live wherever I can find some space and shelter in this big American city. There was no room for me in my mom's place. I can't get food subsidies because I have no fixed address. I can't get a fixed address because I have no job. I can't get a job because I look too unkempt. I can't look neat because I have no place to live. I am waiting. I am waiting for the cycle of poverty to be broken. I am waiting for the Anointed One. Is there really such a one? Will the Messiah come? I am waiting.

Manuel, Rita, Tom, Jane: We are waiting. We are waiting for the Anointed One.

We are waiting for good news for the poor.

We are waiting for release for the captives.

We are waiting for the oppressed to be set free.

Jane: I am Jane. I live in North America. I am a professional, middle-class woman. Until now, I have always been active in my church. My husband is a professional and a church leader. At first I was stunned to silence by my husband's violence. I felt I had failed. I tried harder to please. I went to my pastor. He told me that my husband meant no real harm and that I was to forgive him the beatings even as Christ forgave. He said I must be willing to suffer as Christ suffered. He silenced me. I am waiting. I am waiting to hear the good news. I am waiting to hear of a God of compassion who cares about my suffering. I am waiting for freedom for the oppressed.

Manuel, Rita, Tom, Jane: We are waiting. We are waiting for the Anointed One.

We are waiting for good news for the poor.

We are waiting for release for the captives.

We are waiting for the oppressed to be set free.

[*The on-stage cast remains still as the voices pause.*]

Voice 1: I do not want to hear Mary's song.

Please, Mary, sing your song no more.

Sing your song no more.

[*pause*]

Voice 2: I do not want to hear Jesus' words.

I am like those who heard him that day in the synagogue:

They were filled with rage. They drove him out of town.

I do not want to hear.

Manuel, Rita, Tom, Jane: Why? Why do you not want to hear the song of Mary?

Why? Why do you not want to hear the words of Jesus?

Why?

[*pause*]

Voice 1: Because . . .

Voice 2:	Because . . .
Voices 1 and 2:	Because to hear is to do.
	And he said, "Truly I tell you, just as you did it to one of the least of these who are members of my family, you did it to me."
Voice 2:	Because he said, "Whoever does the will of my Father in heaven is my brother and sister and mother."
Voices 1 and 2:	Because . . .
	[*pause*]
Manuel, Rita:	The Spirit of the Lord is upon me,
Tom, Jane:	because he has anointed me
Manuel, Rita, Tom, Jane:	to bring good news to the poor, to set the oppressed ones free.
	Today this scripture has been fulfilled.
Mary:	My soul magnifies the Lord, and my spirit rejoices in God my Saviour.
All:	We are waiting. Actively waiting.
	The Anointed One is coming.
	The promise is being fulfilled.

Advent Ceremonies for Weeks 2, 3, 4, and Christmas

Advent Ceremony—Week 2 (The Book of Esther)

[*The storyteller stands behind or beside the huge chain that is on the worship table.*] Long ago in the land of Persia the king, King Ahasuerus, decided to have a party. This was a party to end all parties. This party was going to show the world just how rich and powerful he was. The king invited every VIP he could think of and every "wannabee" VIP as well. He totally redecorated the palace. Merchants rubbed their hands with delight as the orders came in for new blue and white curtains and silver couches and goblets of pure gold. The wine sellers scurried about to locate gallons and gallons of the country's finest wines. The party was going to last seven days and everyone was told to drink as much as they wanted. When the last day of the party came, the king had shown off all of his treasures and displayed his wealth and power. He wanted something to be the grand finale, the crowning glory. At last he thought of what it would be. He sent for his wife, Queen Vashti, who was a ravishing beauty. Such a prize would knock their socks off! He sent his eunuchs to her with the message that she was to appear before this stag party and she was to wear the royal crown.

Queen Vashti received the order. She knew what was expected to happen. And she knew that if she did not appear as summoned she may be forfeiting her life. The king was all-powerful. She was powerless. How could she retain her self-respect and her righteousness in the face of such power? She was between the proverbial rock and a hard place. What should she do? She decided to keep her self-respect. She refused the king's order. The king could not bring himself to kill her, but to save face he had to do something; he divorced her, which in those days was just about as devastating. But righteousness won out over misuse of power. Perhaps Mary remembered this event when she sang,

"God has brought down the powerful and lifted up the lowly." God broke the chain of misused power and replaced it with the rainbow of righteousness.

[*The link of the chain is opened and turned to show the second arc of the rainbow, the yellows. This arc is added to the banner as indicated in Week 1 above. The storyteller then continues.*]

We await the coming of Christ who will break the chain of power over others and bring the power of righteousness.

Advent Ceremony—Week 3 (The Gospel of Luke)

[*The storyteller stands behind or beside the huge chain that is on the worship table and tells the story.*] Everybody knew him. He was the least popular man in Jericho. Talk about filling up at the political hog trough—this fellow outdid them all. His job gave him a very comfortable salary but he lusted for more. Gratitude was a word totally foreign to the vocabulary of his life. This man, Zacchaeus, knew how to manipulate the system. The fact that his excess came at the expense of others' hardship did not faze him one bit. What he was doing was legal, wasn't it? One would almost think that he had learned his craft at the feet of some multinational corporation doing a land takeover in a third world country! Anyway, his grasping and accumulating and ingratitude weren't making his life all that satisfying. He decided to hear this teacher, Jesus, speak and see what made him tick. Well, after that

conversation his whole world turned upside-down—actually right-side up. He not only decided that honesty would be his policy, he promised to turn over fifty percent of his holdings to the poor and to pay back four-to-one all the money he had extorted! Now that's gratitude! That's what his encounter with Jesus did. In this man God broke open the chain of ingratitude and replaced it with the rainbow of thankful worship and joyous sharing.

[*The link of the chain is opened and turned to show the third arc, the greens. The arc of greens is added to the banner as indicated in story one above. Then the storyteller continues.*]

We await the Christ who reveals God, God whose love reaches out to us however unworthy.

God who invites a response of obedient action and thankful worship.

Advent Ceremony—Week 4 (1 Samuel 25)

[*The storyteller stands behind or beside the huge chain that is on the worship table.*] The time of sheep shearing had come. This was festival time, party time, a time when people were expected to be hospitable. David knew that his men expected to have a great party. But they were in the fields far from home near the land where Nabal and Abigail lived. Where could he get supplies?

David sent a message to Nabal. He said that not only had he given his shepherds and soldiers instructions not to take Nabal's animals, but he had also instructed his men to guard Nabal's flocks and men from marauding thieves. Therefore, David said, it was a natural request to ask Nabal to give him a few sheep or goats for his festival.

Out of gratitude and out of common courtesy Nabal should have given David some food for his feast. Instead Nabal sent back the message to "get lost," or words to that effect.

This reply so enraged David that he set out with four hundred well-armed young warriors. He spread the word that he intended to kill Nabal and every one of Nabal's sons and menservants. David would show no mercy.

Finally the whole dark story reaches Abigail. She is told of David's request, of her husband's impolite refusal, and of David's threat. She is told that four hundred soldiers are on the way. Abigail has compassion on David. Some of his men and perhaps he himself will be killed. She has compassion on her husband and his men. How can she prevent this merciless bloodshed? She is a powerless woman in a culture where women are considered practically chattel.

In a whirlwind, she swoops into her larder and amasses two hundred loaves of bread, five dressed sheep, five measures of grain, two skins of wine, and two hundred fig cakes and loads them on donkeys. She sends these gifts ahead with two young men. Then she grabs her kerchief and her fastest four-legged Buick and races off to meet David and his four hundred warriors. She is aware that she is not only facing ridicule, she is facing death.

Graciously she convinces David to overlook the foolishness of her husband and to accept the gifts that she offers. The chain of mercilessness is broken by the rainbow of compassion and active peacemaking.

[*Open the link and turn it to show the fourth arc, the blue-indigos. The arc is added to the banner as in the first story. Then the storyteller continues.*]

We await the Christ who reveals a God of compassion who empowers us to be peacemakers.

Christmas Ceremony (Luke 2:1-19)

In place of the Advent ceremony, the storyteller stands in the worship center and tells the Christmas story. God sent the only Son to break the chain of sin.

At the conclusion of the story, the storyteller places a purple circle on the banner, representing the head of the Christ child.

Top-Secret Surprise (choral reading)

Voice 1: Hear ye. Hear ye. Hear ye. Hear the voice of one crying in the wilderness.

Voice 2: Prepare the way of the Lord. Make his paths straight.

Voice 1: Listen, people of God. Hear the good news!

Voices 2, 3: Every valley shall be filled

Voices 4, 5: and every mountain and hill shall be brought low,

Voices 2, 3, 4: the crooked shall be made straight

Voices 3, 4, 5: and the rough ways shall be made smooth;

All voices: [*softly, with confidence and awe*]
and all flesh shall see the salvation of God.

[*pause*]

Voice 1: Listen! Sentinels, lift up your voices. The Lord your Redeemer says:

Voice 2: Just as I swore that the waters of Noah would never again go over the earth,

Voices 2, 3: so I have sworn my steadfast love shall not depart from you.

Voice 1: Break forth into singing, for the Lord has comforted his people.

Voices 3, 4, 5: He is coming to judge the earth with righteousness and the peoples with his truth.

Voice 1: Listen, people of God. Hear the good news:

All voices: He is coming. Coming.
And all flesh shall see the salvation of God.
Hallelujah!

On the Road to Emmaus

Celebrate Easter

Easter begins, like all deep things, in mystery and ends, like all high things, in courage.

—Bliss Perry

In the first two centuries of Christendom, Easter was celebrated by a vigil held from Saturday evening to Sunday dawn. This was a time of blessing of the lamps, scripture readings, songs, sermon, prayers, and Communion. By combining and transforming the Jewish feasts of Pascha and Pentecost, the Easter celebration was a feast of redemption; it celebrated the passion, crucifixion, resurrection, and ascension in one festival. Then, for fifty days after Easter, all acts of penitence, such as fasts and kneeling for prayer, were forbidden. These fifty days were to celebrate the newly baptized members' entrance into the kingdom.

Cyril of Jerusalem, in the fourth century, introduced the idea of commemorating Jesus' passion, death, resurrection, and ascension at their original sites. Subsequently, the celebration of each of these events in the life of Jesus became separated, effectively assigning these events to history as though they only involved ancient people and do not affect our lives today. This allows us to view these events as disinterested onlookers. Our Easter celebration today responds to that concern.

The celebration that follows is a four-act drama in which the members of the congregation are the players. The amaz-ing impact of the truth of Easter cannot be captured in mere words. Ritual is essential in communicating the full meaning of Easter. The Emmaus story is a powerful declaration that both word and sacrament are integral parts of our experience of the presence of Christ.

Bible Text

Luke 24; Mark 16; Matthew 28; John 20; 1 Corinthians 15:1-20a

Bible Background for Our Celebration

Two men in dazzling clothes, standing in the tomb, asked the women in Luke's account, "Why do you look for the living among the dead?" Their question is a sign that everything had changed.

It is interesting that the first people to be told of the resurrection were women. Jesus always affirmed the spiritual insights of women and treated women and men equally. Here God underscores the teaching and action of Jesus and, as in the birth of Jesus, shocks us by breaking free of the accepted culture of the day, in which the testimony of women was not considered valid. Now it was the women who were commissioned to bring the good news to the disciples who were afraid and in hiding. The story does not end there. Resurrection is not the contemplation of the empty tomb; it is the confrontation with a living Christ.

The journey to Emmaus is also our journey. As the two disciples walk dejectedly away from Jerusalem, they are joined by Jesus but do not recognize him. What will it take to enable them or us to see? They may have been told that Jesus is alive, but they have not comprehended the mystery of God's divine cosmic plan. Jesus' explanation of the recent events reveals a God who does not use power and tactics as the Romans do. God rules by the power of redemptive suffering love.

The story includes many ironies: Jesus is the main figure in the story, but he is not recognized; the guest in the home becomes the host; when at last Jesus reveals who he is, he is gone; and it is only in hindsight that the disciples comprehend the meaning of Jesus' teachings on the scriptures.

The story is about presence—the presence of Jesus. The tomb story reveals the absence of the body of Jesus; the Emmaus story proclaims the presence of the living Christ with the people of God. But how is the blindness removed? The experience of the presence of Jesus, made apparent in the act of eating together, enabled them to understand the significance of the scriptural witness. In the breaking of bread, they saw that the suffering of Jesus resulted from his being the Christ of a kingdom of peace, a kingdom not built on military conquest but on forgiving grace.

Like many passages in scripture, this passage functions as a proof of faith. It must be remembered that this scripture was written to a people that already believed in the resurrection. Though at first glance the text moves like a story, we soon see a creedal statement about who Jesus is (Luke 24:19) and a precursor to our Communion ritual (24:30). Luke is doing much more than telling a story or writing history; he is challenging us to allow our faith to compel us to witness.

Faith Nugget

We experience resurrection when we come face-to-face with the living Christ.

Early Preparation

Some preparation for the celebration will need to be done several weeks in advance.

1. Make the Communion bread. Using a sweet dough, as for cinnamon buns, make rolls the size of parker house rolls. These will be put together like sticky buns or *pluckit bread* except that there will be no syrup. Rolling the balls of dough in melted butter before adding them to the baking dish will allow the buns to be broken off easily after baking. Make enough small balls so that each person can break one off for Communion.

2. Ask a handy person to make a standard for the banner. Make the standard from a bamboo pole or other light material and the crossbar from a dowel or a slat with ornate finials (end ornamentation may be made from ribbon, paper mache, or household items). Spray paint with a flat silver paint to look like pewter. The banner may be attached with cloth loops or tacked directly to the crossbar. Have a holder for the standard in place at the worship centre, into which the banner will be placed as part of the procession.

3. Check a local appliance store for a large cardboard carton such as a refrigerator box. Paint it to look like a large boulder and place in front of the opening to the worship area, leaving a space to walk past.

4. Assign leaders for centres and have them gather a list of materials for their activity.

You will need
☐ Communion bread
☐ banner from Advent celebration
☐ banner standard
☐ refrigerator carton
☐ incense

☐ leaders for the Easter centres
☐ actors for the drama
☐ copies of the bulletin and script
☐ trumpeters and other instrumentalists
☐ choir, candles
☐ lilies
☐ a cocoon or picture of one

Name of your church
On the Road to Emmaus
Celebrate Easter

Gathering

Opening Prayer

Getting Ready

Easter Centres

1. Easter Symbols. Learn the Easter symbols, what they mean, and where they come from.
2. Butterflies. Make beautiful butterflies, the symbol of resurrection, for worship.
3. Right-brained Faith. Express your faith artistically, even if you're not an artist.
4. The Emmaus Walk. Come face-to-face with Jesus as you walk.
5. Easter Banner. Create a banner for the procession.
6. Video. See an inspiring video and reflect on its message.
7. Bible Study. Compare the four Gospel accounts of the resurrection.
8. Sing. Sing the hymns that tell the story of Holy Week.

The Easter Celebration

Gathering Again

A Drama in Four Acts

Act 1: The Empty Tomb
Call to Worship
Scripture . . . . Luke 24:1-11
Hymn . . . . "They Crucified My Saviour"
Prayer of Confession
Silent Reflection
Assurance of Pardon . . . . "Because He Lives"

Act 2: Christ Is Risen
Processional
Call to Worship
Invocation
Hymns of Praise
Time with the Children
Hymns

Act 3: Journey to Emmaus
Scripture . . . . Luke 24:13-32
Offerings from the Groups

Act 4: Journey to Jerusalem
Scripture . . . . Luke 24:33-36, 48
Hymn . . . . "At the Lamb's High Feast"
Communion
Pastoral Prayer
Hymn . . . . "Christ Who Left His Home in Glory"
Benediction

The Celebration

Gathering

Open with a resurrection hymn from your hymnal and a prayer that all people gathered in this place will recognize Jesus when they meet him on their walk in life.

Explain to the congregation that just as the women came to prepare Jesus for final burial, everyone will help make preparations for the celebration of Easter. Give instructions for moving to the Easter centres and designate a time for the congregation to regather in the worship place.

Easter Centres

1. Learn the Origins of Easter Symbols. Hand out hymnals and Bibles to old and young alike and ask them to look through the scriptures and songs for symbols of Easter. Add other symbols, such as hot cross buns or eggs. If a set of encyclopaedias is handy, look up the origins of these symbols under "Easter"; also use the information on symbols in the resource section.

Ask people to choose the symbol most meaningful to them and make a drawing of it with markers on a two-inch square piece of mat board or foam centre board. Wrap the edges with copper foil used in making stained glass windows. With a hot glue gun, adhere a safety pin or jewelry clasp to the back and wear as a pin.

2. Change a Clothespin into a Butterfly. Using beautifully coloured tissue paper and clothespins, the kind without the spring, make butterflies for the procession in worship. Give each child or adult two sheets of tissue paper of different colours (about 8.5" by 11") [22cm x 28cm]. Gather the paper at the middle the long way and slide the tissue paper into the clothespin. Follow with the second sheet. Use pipe cleaners for antennae. Attach each butterfly to a looped piece of string. As children carry

them into worship, they should wave their butterflies in the air.

3. Explore a Right-brained Faith. Adults live in a world that values left-brained, logical thinking. But many things about the gospel are not reasonable in a logical sense. The dead live, the poor are rich, and the powerless are powerful. As Christians we need to nourish our spiritual side by suspending logic and thinking a different way. We need to use our senses, our intuition, and artistic expressions to explore all dimensions of faith.

Easter has been a favourite subject for artists. Look in your local library for books on Rembrandt and others who have painted or sculpted the resurrection or Emmaus story. Bring several examples to class. Then ask each person to recall a moment of resurrection in his or her own life, a moment when they met Jesus face-to-face. Since many of us do our best artwork on placemats, napkins, or bulletins (something at our fingertips), hand out scrap paper and have everyone tell their story in sketch or cartoon. Before the end of the period, glue the art pieces to poster board in a collage. Appoint someone to place the collage at the worship during the offering.

4. Take an Emmaus Walk (for youth and adults). Ask participants to reflect on their lives from the earliest they can remember until now. Ask them to recall the times when they felt lost, when they felt confused, when they felt that God was very near to them, when they felt angry with God, when they felt grateful—all the ups and downs of their life journey. Ask them to recall their own resurrection stories. If the weather permits, have them walk outside as they recall this inner journey. If you are confined indoors, give each person a large sheet of art paper and markers to make a time line of their personal faith journey. Be sure to include ups and downs of that journey. Use pictures or symbols to indicate what was going on in various points of the journey. Allow about five minutes each (or more if the group is small) for everyone to tell about their pictures. As they follow the road, encourage them to tell where the journey was dark, who helped them at certain places, how God seemed very near.

5. Make a Banner for Worship. Use the plain blue banner made for Advent, replacing Advent symbols with Easter symbols. From the pattern on page 50, cut the lilies and the cross from felt. Attach Velcro dot fasteners at the edges with hot glue, and arrange the pieces on the banner according to the illustration. Hang the banner from the standard and select one or two people to carry the banner into the celebration.

As you work, talk about the symbolism of the cross. The wooden cross is a symbol of the tree of life. Look at Genesis 3:22-23 for one view of the tree of life. Then look at Revelation 2:7 for another view. The fruit that was forbidden is now offered to us. In combining the tree of life with the lily, Christ becomes the supreme tree that bestows life on us.

6. Watch and Discuss the Video *Light in the Darkness: The Easter Story.* This retelling of the passion story, using mime, masks, and drama, portrays the crucifixion, interspersed with flashbacks of the last week of Jesus' life. You may rent or purchase this fifteen-minute video from EcuFilm by calling 800-251-4091.

7. Biblical Study of the Resurrection (for youth and adults). Count off by fours to make four groups. Provide Bibles for those who didn't bring one. Assign each group one of the four resurrection stories: Matthew 28; Mark 16; Luke 24:1-14; John 20. Ask each group to list on a flip chart the details from each account in the order they happened. When the groups are finished writing, put the sheets up side by side and discuss the similarities and differences between lists. For discussion starters ask why the accounts differ and how the differences in the Gospel accounts make them feel. Uncertain? Mystified? Challenged?

Talk about the significance in the resurrection accounts of anointing; darkness (darkness of Christ's death and the light of resurrection); the stone that is mysteriously rolled away (may signify that we are helpless in the face of death, but God is powerful even in death); the man in the tomb, seated (customary teaching position) on the right (the place of honour), reciting a creedal statement; the man in Mark 14:51-52 who runs away naked.

8. Sing Through the Story of the Passion. Have youth and adults prepare a list of their favourite passion and Easter hymns. Arrange them in order of the events of passion week, and sing them to tell the story of Christ's death and resurrection. Allow time for silent prayer and spoken reflection on people's experience during this the past week.

Gathering Again

The bare white tree that was used to symbolize life at Advent (see "Celebrating Advent") can be reused here in the worship place. Also darken the sanctuary to recreate the darkness of the tomb. Place the painted appliance carton in the doorway, but leave room for people to pass through. Use no Easter decorations. Burn incense to remind people of the spices the women brought to preserve the body of Jesus.

Have the children and adults who will process in at the beginning of Act 2 wait outside the worship area. The rest of the congregation picks up a bulletin/script and enters the darkened area. Only after being seated do they learn that they are the principal players in the four-act drama.

A Drama in Four Acts
Act 1: The Empty Tomb

Call to Worship

Worship Leader: Come, come into the tomb.

See, the door is open

You have come to see where he lay.

He is not here.

Come, see for yourself.
He is not here.

Scripture

Luke 24:1-11

Reader 1 [*read verses 1-3*]

Reader 2 [*read verse 4*]

Reader 1 [*read verses 5-7*]

Reader 2 [*read verses 8-10*]

Reader 1 [*read verse 11*]

Hymn

"They Crucified My Saviour" (p. 51) Sing the four verses without the chorus; they tell of the crucifixion, the entombment, the coming of the women, and the stone rolled away. The chorus, which tells of the resurrection, will be sung later.

Prayer of Confession

One: We confess that, like the Apostles, our fears and doubts keep us behind closed doors.

All: We confess that, like the women, we look for the living among the dead. We fail to understand what we have heard.

One: We confess that, like the apostles, our stereotypes and our prejudices prevent us from hearing the good news.

All: We confess that, like those who walked to Emmaus, we fail to recognize the Christ. We seek a different kind of saviour. We do not like the possibility of suffering.

One: We confess that, unlike the women, we do not always eagerly proclaim the good news. Now, in the silence, hear us, O God.

Silent Reflection

Assurance of Pardon

A soloist or the congregation sings "Because He Lives," also known as "God Sent His Son" (Gaither/Gaither), or other hymn of pardon.

Act 2: Christ Is Risen

Processional

Suddenly all the lights come up. Trumpets begin their fanfare. The procession begins with the banner carrier, the trumpeters, children carrying butterflies, youth carrying potted lilies, and choir members carrying lighted candles, in that order. The choir is singing a processional hymn or one of the anthems listed here. As the parade reaches the worship area, the banner is placed in the standard, the children hang their butterflies on the white tree, the youth place the lilies at the front and on the window sills, the choristers place their candles at the front. The whole church should now be filled with light and sound and scent. The choir remains to sing the Easter anthem and the children and youth find seats with their families.

Suggested anthems: "Awake the Trumpet's Lofty Sound" (Handel); "Look There! The Christ!" (Bennett/Eggert), optional handbells; "Come, Share the Spirit" (Weber), congregation, brass, organ; "Hail the Day That Sees Him Rise" (Powell)

Call to Worship

One: The tomb is empty. Christ is risen.

All: Out of the darkness, hope has been reborn.

One: Like a butterfly born to new life,

All: we are freed to live life in its fullest.

One: Christ is risen.

All: Christ is risen indeed!

One: Come, let us worship and praise the living God!

Worship Leader: Turn to the person nearest you and greet him or her with the words: "Christ is risen!" Respond by saying, "Christ is risen indeed!"

Invocation

God of resurrection love, we come to worship you. Burst open the cocoon of darkness that would imprison us. Defeat the power of sin. Send forth your light that our victorious living may warm the earth and draw others to the joy of the fullness of your presence. Amen.

Hymns of Praise

During the instrumental prelude to the hymn, ushers will give tambourines and similar rhythm instruments to those who will take them. No instruction is necessary.

Suggested hymns: "Lift Your Glad Voices" (Ware/Gould); "Thine Is the Glory" (Burdy/Handel); "O Sons and Daughters, Let Us Sing" (Tisserand/Vulpius)

Time with the Children

Worship Leader: Do you know what this is? [*Show a real cocoon or a picture. Pause for responses.*] Yes, it is a chrysalis. What is inside? It does not seem to be alive. Once it was a larva crawling about like a wriggling worm. Now it is dark and quiet inside. What will come from this? [*pause*] Yes, a butterfly. If we could talk to the larva and tell it all about how one day it would fly, it would not understand. How can you explain flying to a creature that has no idea about what it means to fly. All you could say to it is that someday, at the right time, it will have a new and beautiful body and it will love its new life. Until then, it can enjoy the beautiful life it now has. We all wonder about what happens after we die. We cannot understand that anymore than this chrysalis could understand what it means to be a butterfly. But this one thing we do know. God loves us and whatever God plans for us is good and

beautiful. It is Easter. Today we celebrate again how much God loves us. The eggs you found this morning remind us of the fun we have together and of the food God gives. They also remind us that a new life, a baby chick, comes from an egg. The butterflies you put on the tree tell us about the beautiful earth God has made for us to enjoy and that God will always love us and care for us. God is with us when we are happy and when we are sad. God loves us always.

Hymns

"In the Bulb There Is a Flower" (Sleeth), "Christ Has Arisen" (Olson), or other hymn of resurrection

Act 3: Journey to Emmaus

Scripture

Luke 24:13-32 (for four readers)

Narrator: Now on that same day two [disciples] were going to a village called Emmaus, about seven miles from Jerusalem, and talking with each other about all these things that had happened. While they were talking and discussing, Jesus himself came near and went with them, but their eyes were kept from recognizing him.

Jesus: What are you discussing with each other while you walk along?

Disciple 1: [*looking sad*] Are you the only stranger in Jerusalem who does not know the things that have taken place there in these days?

Jesus: What things?

Disciple 2: The things about Jesus of Nazareth, who was a prophet mighty in deed and word before God and all the people, and how our chief priests and leaders handed him over to be condemned to death and crucified him. But we had hoped that he was the one to redeem Israel.

Disciple 1: Yes, and besides all this, it is now the third day since these things took place. Moreover, some women of our group astounded us. They were at the tomb early this morning, and when they did not find his body there, they came back and told us that they had indeed seen a vision of angels who said that he was alive. Some of those who were with us went to the tomb and found it just as the women had said; but they did not see him.

Jesus: Oh, how foolish you are, and how slow of heart to believe all that the prophets have declared! Was it not necessary that the Messiah should suffer these things and then enter into his glory?

Narrator: Then beginning with Moses and all the prophets, he interpreted to them the things about himself in all the scriptures. [*Jesus begins to walk away from the disciples*.]

Disciple 1: Stay with us, because it is almost evening and the day is now nearly over.

Narrator: [*as Jesus turns back to them*] So he went in to stay with them. When he was at the table with them, he took bread, blessed and broke it, and gave it to them.

[*As the disciples suddenly show signs of recognizing Jesus, he vanishes from them.*]

Disciple 2: Were not our hearts burning within us, while he was talking to us on the road, while he was opening the scriptures to us?

Offering

Worship Leader: In preparation for this celebration, we have been on our own journey to Emmaus. Through art, symbol, study, and music, we have come face-to-face with the risen Lord. During this time of offering, we invite those who made visual images of Easter to bring them to the worship table along with our monetary offerings, so that others may see them. As we bring our offerings forward, the music group will lead us in singing some of the hymns of passion and Easter.

[*If you do not have a music group, have the organist or pianist play a selection of Easter hymns.*]

Act 4: Journey to Jerusalem

Scripture

Luke 24:33-36, 48

Worship Leader: Peace be with you. Christ is risen. Christ is risen indeed! We celebrate the presence of the living Lord. God is with us. God is among us.

Hymn

"At the Lamb's High Feast" or other Communion hymn

Communion

Worship Leader: The bread we receive today is sweet and generous to remind us of God's lavish gift of eternal life now and of the great feast that is to come. [*Pass just the bread. When all have received a piece, say the Lord's Prayer together and eat.*]

Pastoral Prayer

Hymn

"Christ Who Left His Home in Glory" (Kolb) or other benediction hymn

Benediction

One: Christ is risen!

All: Christ is risen indeed!

Resources for This Celebration

Centre 1. Easter Symbols

The pomegranate (Num. 13:23; Exod. 28:33-34). This Old Testament symbol was adopted by Christianity where the bursting of the fruit and release of seeds became a symbol of the resurrection.

The peacock. When persecutions of the church made it necessary for Christians to hide the dead, grave diggers who were a minor clergy, dug what we call the catacombs. The entrance to most of the catacombs was near or in a church. It is said that the length of the underground tunnels of the catacombs was about 587 miles. Some were well cut, with wide passages, some narrow with a look of architecture, some were rude undecorated tunnels. Symbols and pictures found in the catacombs include: the Greek monogram of Christ, Christ as Good Shepherd, woman in prayer, dove, peacock, and pelican. The cross was not used. The peacock was a borrowed symbol for immortality. It was sacred to Juno. It is said that a peacock was released at the funeral of an empress to signify her deification.

The tree of life (Gen. 3:22-23; Rev. 2:7; 22:2, 5; John 8:12). In the Adam and Eve story, the fruit of the tree was forbidden to the couple. In Revelation we are invited to take freely from the tree. The tree of life also has a part in the Easter story. The wooden cross made from a tree brings death to Jesus, but it is also the tree of life from which life springs anew.

Wheat (John 12:23-24; 1 Cor. 15:35-37, 42). Jesus says that, like the kernel of wheat that must "die" and be buried in the soil in order to germinate, he must lose his life to gain it. Moreover, all of us must lose our lives to gain life.

Crocus (Isa. 35:1-4). Isaiah uses the crocus flower, which blooms in the arid Middle Eastern desert, to signify new life from death, just as we experience new life from the sacrificial death of Jesus. In snowy climates, the crocus is one of the first flowers to emerge in the spring, often coming up through the snow that blankets the "dead" earth through the winter.

They Crucified My Saviour

1 They cru-ci-fied my Sav-ior and nailed him to the cross. They cru-ci-fied my Sav-ior and nailed him to the cross, and the Lord will bear my spir-it home.

2 Jo-seph begged his bod-y and laid it in the tomb. Jo-seph begged his bod-y and laid it in the tomb, and the Lord will bear my spir-it home.

3 Ma-ry, she came run-ning, a-look-ing for my Lord. Ma-ry, she came run-ning, a-look-ing for my Lord, and the Lord will bear my spir-it home.

4 An an-gel came from heav-en and rolled the stone a-way. An an-gel came from heav-en and rolled the stone a-way, and the Lord will bear my spir-it home.

African American Spiritual

Coming Together, Going Out

Celebrate Pentecost

The church is a modern miracle.

Where else could a traitor (Matthew the tax collector) and a superpatriot (Simon the zealot) be a part of the same group? Unlike a club, which is made up of like-minded people, the church is a family of different people united by the Spirit in a common purpose.

Ask the average church school class of twelve-year-olds about church celebrations and they will tell you about Christmas and Easter and Thanksgiving. Mention Pentecost and you often draw a blank. Why is this significant festival so under celebrated? Perhaps it is because we have difficulty connecting the biblical events with the experience of our own lives and also with the life of the church. We have not seen tongues of fire above our heads as we worship. We find the events recorded in Acts confusing and perhaps even incomprehensible and troubling. How can we make this important festival part of the practice of our faith?

The celebration of Pentecost, when thousands were converted in a day by the Holy Spirit, intensifies the importance of our decision to become followers of Christ. For not only did we experience the grace of God in that moment; we were thrust into an exciting mission.

The festival itself comes from the Old Testament. Names given to this harvest celebration in the Old Testament (NRSV) include the festival of weeks (Exod. 16:10; Num. 28:26), the festival of harvest (Exod. 23:16), and the day of first fruits (Num. 28:26; Exod. 23:16; 34:22). Since the celebration was commemorated on the fiftieth day after the beginning of the harvest, it became known as

Pentecost, a Greek term meaning "fiftieth day." The first crop of the season, barley, ripened in Palestine in April, with wheat ripening somewhat later. In the cooler hill country, the harvest was not ready until late May or early June. The seven-week period was sure to encompass the entire harvest period before the celebration.

This Old Testament harvest festival was itself a combination of several other festivals. In addition to a harvest celebration, it was a time to give thanks to God. It was a time to celebrate the receiving of the law at Mount Sinai. In fact, the thunder and lightning on the mountain when the law was given to Moses is symbolized in the wind and fire of the New Testament account of Pentecost. The alienation and loss of community in the tower of Babel story is overcome in the Pentecost experience in which understanding and the community of believers are restored. The unity that God desires is based not on common language or common goals, but on a common commitment to do God's will.

In the Old Testament, wind and fire are two powerful symbols of the presence of God. The New Testament reminds us that just as God's Spirit was poured out in previous times of re-birth and renewal, so it is now with the birth of the church. All barriers are overcome; gender, race, and nationality no longer alienate us. All are filled with the indwelling power of the Holy Spirit to be sent forth as God's witnesses. God's presence continues to be with us, in us and among us, comforting and empowering.

Bible Text

Acts 2:1-42 [Psalm 67:5-7; Psalm 95:6; Exodus 20:1-17; Deuteronomy 9:9-11; 16:9-12; Leviticus 23:15-16]

Biblical Background for Our Festival

In Acts 2 we are given three statements about the Holy Spirit: the Holy Spirit is given by God; the Holy Spirit is given to the community of faith; the Holy Spirit is given to enable the church in mission.

The Holy Spirit is not earned or deserved, nor is it a reward for special righteousness. The followers who had gathered at Jerusalem were not there to seek this gift. They were in a position to receive and respond but not to bring about the giving of this gift. Secondly, it is important to note that the gift of the Holy Spirit is given to the community of faith, not to individuals. There had been division in Jerusalem. Those gathered were of many nations and many interpretations. The Holy Spirit brought unity in the midst of this diversity and came to the individual only in that the individual was part of this diverse community of faith. And, thirdly, the Holy Spirit is given so that the church can ful-fill its mission: to reach out to all peoples in all nations.

When the Holy Spirit rushed in, the people heard in their own language. When we fail to hear each other, even when we speak the same language, we fail to be in relationship with each other. It is God who enables peoples of all cultures to hear each other and to be in relationship.

Luke, the probable author of Acts, would keep us from privatizing and trivializing the gift of the Holy Spirit by reminding us that the works of God are being seen and heard and believed everywhere. There is no exclusive club that can claim it alone knows the Holy Spirit. And the indwelling of the Holy Spirit signals more than mere acceptance; it invites us to be a part of the people of this new covenant with a mission to do Christ's work. That is at once a joyous and sobering prospect.

Long before Pentecost, this universality had been spoken of in the scriptures, but obviously the people did not fully understand. Psalm 67 is one such scripture where the Bible talks about the universality of redemption. In the psalm, Israel's tendency to exclude people of other nations and press for purity is replaced with a new passion, a desire to make all nations the people of God. God has reaped a bountiful harvest of peoples and nations. We return our thanks in worship and service to God's people.

Faith Nugget

The Holy Spirit comes to unify us and send us out on a common mission.

Early Preparation

This festival, unlike others in this book, does not have activity centres. It is a festival that tries to capture in modern terms the spirit of the original event. Through drama, music, and prayer, the festival recreates a feeling of unification and inspiration to go out together in witness.

The planning group should meet four to six weeks ahead to make decisions, issue invitations, and promote the festival in church publications.

1. Six weeks before Pentecost, begin rehearsal of the drama.

2. Four weeks before the festival, begin work on the music, give scripts to the readers, and give material to the people doing the Time with the Children.

3. Three weeks in advance, prepare the streamers and hurricane lamp.

4. One week before, include in the bulletin the suggestion that people wear red on the next Sunday, Pentecost Sunday. It may be red clothing or something with red in it or a red lapel flower, for example. The bulletin should also announce that the service will not have separate Sunday school classes that day and that the festival will include the children and people of all ages. Be sure to include the usual times for your worship and study.

5. On Saturday before the festival, put the red flowers and lamp in place. Have stools available for the Time with the Children.

Note: Remind the worship leader to leave a time for silent reflection and confession. Too often this is included in the bulletin but an actual time is not given during the service. Have the worship leader actually allow a minimum of sixty seconds for this.

You will need
- ❏ invitations
- ❏ copies of the script for participants
- ❏ actors
- ❏ stools
- ❏ red flowers
- ❏ red, orange, and yellow streamers
- ❏ hurricane lamp
- ❏ red crayons
- ❏ white strips of paper

Name of your church
Coming Together, Going Out
Celebrate Pentecost

Call to Worship

Invocation

Anthem . . . . "Holy Spirit, Come with Power"

Hymn . . . . "The God of Abraham, Praise"

Prayer of Confession

Scripture . . . . Acts 2:1-39 [selected readings]

Message . . . . "Four Solos and a Quintette"

Solo . . . . "Like the Murmur of the Dove's Song"

Anthem . . . . "Through Our Fragmentary Prayers"

Congregational Prayer and Choral Response . . . . . "Hear Our Prayer"

Time with the Children

Children's Hymn . . . . "Spirit of God"

Offering Hymn . . . . "For the Fruit of All Creation"

Offering

Unity Circle

Hymns of Praise and Joy

Benediction

Recessional Hymn . . . . "You Shall Go Out with Joy"

The Festival

Place many red flowers around the worship area. Also, use one or more large hurricane lamps with red glass chimneys or chimneys painted red. The flickering red flames remind us of the tongues of flame at Pentecost.

As the children enter the service, the ushers give each a red crayon and a strip of white paper (2" x 20" or 5cm x 50 cm). The following should be printed in block letters on each strip of paper: I,_____, AM A CHILD OF GOD. The ushers tell the children to print their names, colour the letters, decorate the paper, and take the slips to the children's time.

Call to Worship

One: Hear the good news: The law of the Lord is perfect,

All: reviving the soul.

One: The decrees of the Lord are sure,

All: making wise the simple.

One: More to be desired than gold,

All: Sweeter than the drippings of the honeycomb.

One: We remember what God has done. Come let us worship.

All: We come, remembering how God's Spirit came as wind and fire.

One: We come, knowing that the Spirit of God continues to move among us.

Acts 2:1-39

Narrator: When the day of Pentecost had come, they were all together in one place.

[Streamer bearers enter and pass through the congregation.]

And suddenly, from heaven there came a sound like the rush of a violent wind, and it filled the entire house where they were sitting. Divided tongues, as of fire, appeared among them, and a tongue rested on each of them. All of them were filled with the Holy Spirit and began to speak in other languages, as the Spirit gave them ability.

Readers 1, 2, 3: *[speaking in their respective languages, slowly and distinctly]* Dear God, what is happening to us? Your presence rushes in upon us like we have never felt before. What are we to make of it? Should we be frightened or overjoyed? Is this the end of the world or the beginning?

Narrator: At this sound, the crowd gathered and was bewildered, because each one heard them speaking in the native language of each. Amazed and

astonished, they asked, "Are not all of these who are speaking Galileans? And how is it that we hear in our own language? English, Spanish, German? [*name appropriate languages*] All were amazed and perplexed, saying to one another:

Reader 4: What does this mean?

Narrator: Hear the words of the prophet Joel.

Reader 1: *[reads Acts 2:17-21]*

Narrator: Peter spoke, saying:

Reader 2: God raised Jesus up, having freed him from death, because it was impossible for him to be held in its power. God raised Jesus up, and of that all of us are witnesses. Repent and be baptized every one of you, in the name of Jesus Christ, so that your sins may be forgiven; and you will receive the gift of the Holy Spirit. For the promise is for you, for your children, and for all who are far away, everyone whom the Lord our God calls.

All: Come, let us worship and serve God.

Invocation

Anthem

"Holy Spirit, Come with Power" (Rupp/White) or other invocation hymn

Hymn of Praise

"The God of Abraham, Praise" (Jewish doxology)

Prayer of Confession

Sing a confessional hymn such as "We Come As Kindling for the Fire" (Huber/Tallis). Pause between verses to reflect on the words of the hymn and pray.

Scripture

Selections from Acts 2:1-39 (see the box on page 56). For this reading you will need five readers, two of whom speak languages other than English. You should use the languages spoken by people in your congregation.

You will also need a number of people (1 for every 10-20 people present) to pass through the worship area with red, orange, and yellow streamers to simulate the coming of the Holy Spirit. Several streamers (1 metre or 1 yard in length) can be affixed to the end of a stick or dowel. Encourage streamer bearers to wave the streamers through the air in large circles and figure eights to represent the tongues of fire. If you are meeting outdoors, appoint youth to wave lighted sparklers to create smoke and fire. Still others can wave incense sticks.

Message
Four Solos and a Quintette

The script for this drama is found on pages 61 - 65. No costumes are needed, but rehearse several weeks ahead and collect the few props you will need. Note that the streamer bearers will have a part in the drama also.

Solo

Soloist sings "Like the Murmur of the Dove's Song" (Daw/Cutts) or other response hymn or song.

The soft and gentle unaccompanied solo breaks into the silence.

Anthem

With only a slight pause after the solo, the choir sings "Through Our Fragmentary Prayers" (Berthier) or other prayer hymn.

Congregational Prayer

Where a response is indicated, the leader asks the congregation to join with the choir in singing "Hear Our Prayer" ("Oyenos, Mi Dios") by Alstott/Hurd or "Lord, Listen to Your Children Praying" (Medema) or other prayer response.

Leader: Let us offer our prayers to God. Creating God, your Spirit brooded over the chaos and the world was created; you fashioned us in your image and breathed into us life. When we turned away from you, your Spirit called the prophets and empowered them to speak your word to us. You gave us your Son. The Spirit descended like a dove at Jordan and as tongues of fire at Pentecost. For all of these gracious gifts, we offer our thanks. Visit our congregation as you did the congregation at that first Pentecost. Like a gust of wind, blow out the dry, dusty leaves that keep us crackling with old prejudices and empty concepts. Like tongues of fire, kindle our vision and hope and commitment. By your love, bind us together, Lord.

We hear your Spirit groan with our spirit for an end to war and all of suffering. We grieve for those who suffer violence. Speak to the leaders of the nations and call them to peace and justice and righteousness. [*Response*]

Leader: For our own nation and its leaders we pray. [*Response*]

Leader: For your church throughout the world, we pray. May it be a light, a mighty force of love and justice and healing. [*Response*]

Leader: For this congregation we pray. Send us love, send us power, send us grace.

We pray for the people sitting in front of us [*pause*], for those sitting behind us [*pause*] for those sitting beside us [*pause*]. For those who are dying, we pray [*pause*]. For those who long to die, we pray [*pause*]. For those who grieve, and for the unemployed. [*Response*]

Leader: We offer our supplications. We offer our thanks to you [*pause*]. May your Spirit dance joy into our lives and fill us with power and courage. Scatter us like life-giving seed to be your witnesses to the ends of the earth. Your kingdom come, O God, your will be done. Amen.

Time with the Children

As children come to the worship area, three youth or adults also approach. Each has a stapler or roll of cellophane tape. As the adults turn the slips of paper into headbands for each child, the pastor or adult helper places a headband on a child's head and says, "Pentecost is the day that God brought us all together as one family and gave us a job to do. We are going to bless each one of you as a member of this family and give you something to do for God." To each individually, the adult says:

"_____(name)_____, you are a child of God. God loves you. God wants you to love others."

When all of the children are wearing their headbands, an adult explains to the children that they will worship God. Each time they hear the following words, they may make the motion or sound that goes with it.

Creator/create: Slap hands together as if modelling something of clay.

Maker/make: Click your tongue.

Wind: Say "whooooooo."

Fire: Spin around once quickly.

Breathe/breath: Say "swishshsh."

Love: Cross your arms over your heart.

Then the adults will present the following reading and lead the children in making motions and sound effects when they hear the key words.

Reader 1: In the beginning when God created [*slap*] the heavens and the earth, the earth had no form and darkness covered the face of the waters.

Reader 2: The wind [*whooooooo*] of God blew and blew. God created [*slap*] the stars. God made [*click*] the planets. The wind [*whooooooo*] blew and there was light. The wind [*whooooooo*] blew and fire [*spin*] danced from the face of the sun and the earth grew warm.

Reader 1: And God made [*click*] people, women and men.

Reader 2: And God breathed [*swishshsh*] into them the breath [*swishshsh*] of life. They were so thrilled to have life that they danced like flames of fire [*spin*].

Reader 1: From the beginning, God's Spirit brought life and joy. Then God sent Jesus into the world to show us how to live. His life showed the Spirit of God. When Jesus was gone, the followers wondered, "Who will show us God's way?" They were all together in Jerusalem when, suddenly, it seemed like there was a great wind [*whooooo*]. It was just as though tongues of crackling fire [*spin*] had come.

Reader 2: And the people knew that God had made [*click*] them into the church. God had created [*slap*] a bond of love [*arms over heart*] among them. They wanted to love [*arms over heart*] each other. They wanted to live as Jesus lived. They wanted to tell others about God. Some of them said, "It is like a birthday! It is the birthday of the church."

[*Point to the burning candle*] The fire [*spin*] in the candle reminds us of the love [*arms over heart*] God has for us and the love [*arms over heart*] we have for God. The fire [*spin*] of the candle reminds us to love [*arms over heart*] others. The fire [*spin*] of the candle reminds us that the church, you and I, do the work of God in the world. Go now, remembering that you are a child of God. God loves you.

Children's Hymn

"Spirit of God" (Medical Mission Sisters) or other favourite children's hymn

Offering Hymn

"For the Fruit of All Creation" (Green/ Lehman) or other Pentecost hymn

Offering

Worship Leader: You are invited to bring your offering to the front. Whether or not you have a monetary offering, you are invited to bring your offering between your hands in the same manner that the actors gave the gift to you. The invisible gift you bring may be whatever you wish to offer to God. Only you and God will know what it is. Please take your hymnal with you. Instead of returning to your seats after the offering, form a large circle around the worship area. [*The actors should respond first, as examples for the congregation. This is an opportunity for lively instrumental music to encourage people to bring their gifts with joy.*]

Hymns of Praise and Joy

Sing several of the following or choose praise hymns from your hymnal or songbook. Consider having liturgical dancers interpret the hymns as the congregation hums the melody.

"Move in Our Midst" (Morse/Huffaker)
"O Holy Spirit, Making Whole"
	(Tweedy/Dykes)
"O Holy Spirit, Root of Life"
	(Janzen/Enns)
"Jubilate Deo Omnis Terra" (Berthier)
"Like David the Shepherd, I Sing"

Benediction

Worship Leader: Go now, remembering what has happened in this place,

And may the winds of the Spirit give you strength and courage to live fully and joyfully,

May the fire of the Spirit give you blazing zeal to spread forth the good news,

May the love of the Spirit send you into the world as the Body of Christ.

God's grace and peace be with you all. Amen.

Recessional Hymn

"You Shall Go Out with Joy"
	(Rubin/Dauermann)

The choir will lead the procession out, followed by the actors, who carry out the red flowers from the front. Actors motion to the people, inviting them to follow them out singing. Some distance from the worship area, the actors turn and hand out the red flowers randomly to the congregation. The singing continues until the congregation has exited.

Four Solos and a Quintette

A one-act drama for Pentecost

CAST

Bryce: Twenty-something. Long hair. Logical, math type. Quiet humour.

Tanya: Early forties. Serious. Theologically trained.

Mike: Fortyish. Sports fan. Pessimist. Lacks generosity.

Cheryl: Thirty. Spirited. Generous good humor.

Narrator

Young Girl

PRODUCTION NOTES: No special staging or costumes are needed. Each actor carries a rake and a Walkman tape player. Provide four tapes of instrumental music: classical, country, easy listening, and rock.

SETTING: A community park. Actors enter individually from various entrances.

Narrator: After a discussion on missions outreach and civic involvement, Second Christian Church made a decision to have some of its members rake the community park. The names of four people were drawn for the job. Here they come.

[*The actors straggle in from various entrances and greet each other briefly.*]

Bryce: [*Enters last. Looks at watch.*]

Well, it's nine o'clock. I guess it's time to get at it. This is definitely not a job that I'd choose.

Cheryl: [*laughs*] Who chose? We were chosen. [*Pause*] Hey. Think of that! We're the chosen ones!

Mike: I wonder if it really was just luck. It doesn't look accidental to me.

Tanya: Why do you say that? What do you mean?

Mike: Look at us. We're all able-bodied. [*Looks at others critically.*] Well, more or less.

[*Bryce smiles and holds up his arm to indicate a very small muscle and mimes weakness.*]

What if Jamie's name had been drawn—he with his broken ankle? Or old Sara Bingham?

Cheryl: Their names would not have been put in the same box as ours, the . . .

Mike: [*with a sarcastic laugh*] That's what I'm saying. The whole thing is rigged.

Bryce: [*gently, with a smile*] Yea, well, here we are.

Mike: Okay, but I'm putting on my tape. [*He removes his tape player from his jacket pocket.*]

Bryce: You brought some music. Good man! So did I. [*He takes out his player.*] What have you got?

Mike: [*names his easy listening music and plays a bit of it*]

Bryce: Hmm. [*gently*] Elevator music.

Mike: You don't like it?

Bryce: It's not my type of music, that's all.

Tanya: What have you got there, Bryce?

Bryce: [*brightly*] Listen to this! [*He names his rock and roll music and plays some of it.*]

Mike: [*interrupting the music*] That's music? That's noise!

Bryce: [*good naturedly*] Noise! Listen to those intricate chord changes. Incredible! And the beat will make us rake faster.

Mike: Yea, to get away from it.

[*The two women have taken out their tapes.*]

Bryce: Let's hear what the women brought. What's your tape, Tanya?

Tanya: [*names and plays her classical music*] Pachelbel's *Canon in D Major.*

Bryce: Classical. Should have guessed that. And yours, Cheryl?

Cheryl: Simple, good old relationship songs for me. Country music. Things might be desperate but you can always sing about it. [*Plays some.*]

Bryce: Well, it does have a beat.

Mike: Forget the music. We came here to rake.

[*Actors move to the four corners to rake.*]

Cheryl: We're really lucky there's no wind today.

Tanya: Yes, it's very still, isn't it? A perfect day.

Mike: [*checking the sky*] Probably the calm before the storm. We're about due for a summer storm. Just our luck to be caught in one.

Tanya: [*to Cheryl*] There's not a dark cloud in the sky. Where does he see a storm?

[*They all continue to rake in silence for a few moments.*]

Cheryl: [*stops raking and follows the flight of an imaginary leaf fluttering in the breeze*] Look at that! Where'd that come from?

Tanya: What? What are you talking about?

Cheryl: Did you see that leaf fluttering? Did you see how long it stayed up?

Tanya: You never saw a leaf before?

Cheryl: Yea. I've seen leaves float about before. But we just got done saying there's no breeze today. Can you feel any breeze?

Tanya and
Cheryl: [*together*] Look. [*They both follow the flight of another leaf.*]

Cheryl: It's like the Spirit. The Holy Spirit. Things are suddenly moving. [*Pauses*] I often wonder about the day all those Jewish-Christians were gathered together and they heard in their own language. I've never understood that. Have you?

Tanya: I think it's like our music. When we each play our own tapes and listen to our own kind of music, we express different moods.

Cheryl: Yes. I'm not a rock fan, Bryce. But your music did put me in an energetic mood. I would say it had an exciting spirit to it.

Mike: I'd have to admit that. Maybe I shouldn't have labelled it noise. It's just that I'm not used to this rock stuff and that's how it seems to me, noise.

Bryce: And your music, Mike, even though I called it elevator music, it did have a spirit of serenity. It was soothing.

Tanya: Your country music has a spirit of optimism, Cheryl.

Mike: And Tanya's classical music gives me grand thoughts.

Bryce: Yes, a spirit of hope and of something beyond ourselves. The same is true of people. You know, like when you hear a man like Nelson Mandela speak, for instance—the man exudes a spirit of hope and reconciliation. Or Mother Teresa. She generates a spirit of peace and contentment.

Tanya: We each brought our own music. We each bring our own gifts to the whole. What kind of spirit do you think Jesus showed?

Cheryl: The easiest answer to that is, Jesus showed the Spirit of God.

Mike: We're back to the Holy Spirit again. Who, what, where is the Holy Spirit?

Tanya: We're back to the breeze that started all this. We did not see it. But we did see what the breeze did. We watched the leaves take flight and glide and skip.

Bryce: And sometimes it is not a gentle breeze. Sometimes its a wind we'd rather not have at all. Or at least that's what we think at the time. Sometimes the old is uprooted. Sometimes the wind causes upheaval and change.

Cheryl: If we allow the Spirit to control our lives, then . . . ?

Tanya: Then we radiate the Spirit of Christ.

Bryce: Scary. Our responsibility, I mean—to reflect Christ.

Mike: And yet each of us does this in our own unique way, don't we? Each of us plays our own music.

Cheryl: You know, I think we have just seen some work of the Holy Spirit.

Bryce: [aside] She's seen another leaf.

Cheryl: When we got here this morning we were not very eager to carry out this project. And we each intended to work alone. No, we did not each say that, but we did come with our individual headsets, didn't we? We also made it fairly clear that we did not think much of each other's taste in music.

Tanya: And now?

Cheryl: And now I think we would each listen to all of the music. Wouldn't we?

Others: That's true. Yea. Uh huh. Sure.

Mike: So you're saying that one aspect of the Spirit's work is to bring us together.

Tanya: The Spirit makes us one body. Yes. The Holy Spirit makes Christ personal and the Holy Spirit creates community.

Mike: I get a little nervous when people start up about the Spirit. Some of these people talk as though they have a corner on the Spirit.

Bryce: I agree. The worst times in history are when certain people claim they alone have communicated with God and know the truth. I'd rather hear about a spirit who is a comforter, guide, healer—words like that.

Tanya: Those are all good names for the Holy Spirit. But the Holy Spirit also pricks the conscience. It brings us face-to-face with the reality of the emptiness of our lives and challenges us to commitment.

Cheryl: I think it's like the leaves we saw blowing. You "know" by the result. The sign of the Spirit is the fruit: love, joy, peace, patience . . .

Mike: kindness, goodness, faithfulness . . .

Bryce: gentleness, self-control . . . joy . . . I know you said "joy" Cheryl, but I just had to say it again because . . .

[*Suddenly, out of nowhere, a young girl skips onto the stage. She may have been sitting in the front pew; she must come as a sudden and complete surprise. The girl comes before Bryce. She is holding her hands together as though she is holding a hidden object in them. She offers it to Bryce who holds out both hands to receive the imaginary gift. She puts the gift in his hands and closes his fingers over it. She does this to each one. While the actors are standing there looking at their closed, outstretched hands, she disappears.*]

Bryce: Where did she come from?

Cheryl: Where did she go?

Tanya: What did she give?

[*They open their hands, hold them out, and begin to laugh. Then the actors go to the four corners of the sanctuary.*]

Bryce: [*standing at the end of the pew*] Please stand. [*When the congregation is standing and everyone is silent, he continues.*] When you are given this gift, please receive it prayerfully. Then pass it on to the person beside you and repeat what is said to you. Then please sit down and listen in silence.

[*All four actors now do and say the same thing. If the church is large, you may have to enlist others who have practiced what to do. These extras will be seated at the ends of pews as required.*]

Actors: The gift of the Spirit is already yours.

[*Mime giving a gift to the person at the end of the pew. Just as the girl did, close their hands over the gift but before you close their hands, blow gently on them. While this happens, the people with the coloured streamers go along each row letting the streamers lightly touch the heads of the people in the congregation. Throughout the church the murmur of people repeating the phrase will be heard. Then there will be silence. Wait until there is complete silence.*]

The Household of Faith

Celebrate the Family of God

6

> As God's chosen ones, holy and beloved, clothe yourselves with compassion, kindness, humility, meekness, and patience. Above all, clothe yourselves with love, which binds everything together in perfect harmony.
>
> *—Colossians 3:12, 14*

Paul was one of the earliest Christians to attempt to find a metaphor for the church. After exploring various images, he settled for the image of the church as a living body. Since then people have suggested many other images. Some have said that the church is like a university where we learn together and then share our knowledge with others. Others have viewed the church as a hospital where the sick come to be healed. Another definition sees the church as an army waging a war of faith against sin and evil. All of these images of the church have validity. No one image can encompass the concept of the church completely.

Today we will look at the church as a household or a family. We are using the word *household* because for some the family may be a group home, for others it may be a number of adult siblings living together, still others may live in an intentional community, and so forth. Regardless of any biological relationship, these groups relate together as family. We celebrate that the members of the church are in a relationship that is akin to a family relationship.

Bible Text

Colossians 3:12-17; Ephesians 1:3—4:16; Mark 3:31-35; 2 Timothy 3:10-17

Bible Background for Our Celebration

The writer to the church at Ephesus, in one Greek sentence, gives us three major themes: the centrality of Christ, the certainty of God's will, and the surety of God's grace. For whom, we might ask. For whom is Christ central, authoritative, and graceful? Jesus is these things for the church, for the people who are made in the image of God and adopted into the family of God, to be united under the leadership of Christ. Jesus had stated this in simple and direct language when he looked over his followers and remarked: "Here are my mother and my brothers. Whoever does the will of God is my brother and sister and mother."

This is the church: those who do the will of God. How then are we sisters and brothers, father and mother, family to each other? In a letter Paul reminds Timothy that he (Timothy) learned his faith from his grandmother and mother, Lois and Eunice, and now is learning from Paul. Like a family member, Paul has been a model for

young Timothy to follow. Paul exemplified a life of faith, patience, love, and steadfastness for his brother in Christ. Like Paul, we can be faithful family to each other as we model the Christian faith for others.

Faithful living as the family of God is spelled out in more detail in the letter to the church at Colossae. The writer reminds the church that as God's chosen ones they are to be kind, forgiving, bearing each other's burdens, teaching one another and, above all, showing love to one another.

As we are led by Christ, living in unity as the obedient and loving children of God, we are the household of God, the church family. With the psalmist we too can say, "How lovely is your dwelling place . . . " (84:1). With the psalmist we also recognize that while a day in the temple brings untold happiness, the utmost happiness comes to "those who walk uprightly" (84:11).

Faith Nugget

The church is not a collection of individuals; it is a family in which we encourage and admonish each other as brothers and sisters in the Christian journey.

Early Preparation

1. Select and meet with all group leaders to give them information and decide on the rooms for each centre. Have them gather the needed materials.

2. Prepare the banner and the "stones," and select the banner carriers.

3. Select the people to present the message and give them the material.

4. Give the musicians the chosen hymns.

5. In the bulletin, for several Sundays in advance, remind members of the congregation to bring sack lunches for this celebration. You may wish to have a committee prepare dessert and beverage for everyone.

You will need

- ❑ stones cut from gray or brown construction paper
- ❑ banner with a house outline
- ❑ slips of paper with table numbers on them for each participant
- ❑ number placards for each table
- ❑ ten or twelve crayons per table
- ❑ paper-covered tables
- ❑ dessert and beverage

The Household of Faith

Celebrate the Family of God

The Celebration

Call to Celebrate

Invocation

Hymns of Praise . . . . . . "God of the Earth,
the Sky, the Sea"
"Praise the Lord"

Hymn of Confession. . . . "Where Charity
and Love Prevail"

Prayer of Confession

Silent Reflection

Assurance of Pardon

Time with the Children

Children's Hymn. . . . . "There's a
Quiet Understanding"

Scripture . . . . Ephesians 1:3-6
Mark 3:31-35
2 Timothy 3:10, 14-15
Colossians 3:12-17

Message . . . . "On Being the
Household of Faith"

Hymn . . . . "Help Us to
Help Each Other"

Family Centres

1. Brothers and Sisters. A fun way to get to know one another through Bible study.
2. Working Together. Play a game to find out about cooperation.
3. The Healing Family. Talk about personal healing for physical and emotional disease.
4. Created in God's Image. Find out what it means to be created in God's image and to be God's helper.
5. The Family that Plays Together. Little children and adults learn games from each other.
6. Putting Out the Welcome Mat. Look for the welcome signs at our church.
7. Creating Family Rituals and Customs. Examine the customs and traditions of the church family.
8. Make Music Together. All ages make music together about families.

Gathering Again

Gathering Music . . . . "Will You Let
Me Be Your Servant"

Affirmation of Faith

Pastoral Prayer

Offering

Hymn of Commission. . . . . . . "For Christ
and the Church"

Benediction

Family Reunion

The Celebration

In the foyer hang a large banner on a standard. On the banner is the outline of a house (see p. 77). The words "The Church—God's Household" appear above and below the house. Station people near the entrance to hand out stones cut from gray or brown construction paper. As people enter, helpers will ask someone in each household to place a stone on the house for every member of the household. When everyone has entered, the house will be "built" completely of stones. Appoint someone to carry the banner into the worship area at the beginning of the celebration. The choir will process in behind the banner, singing "Living Stones" or another processional hymn about the church or family of God.

Call to Celebrate

Worship Leader: The church has been likened to a university where we come to learn and go out to share. It has been likened to a bank where we come to draw strength. Others have called the church an army of faith that fights evil. Paul used the metaphor of the body. All of these metaphors have something to say to us. Today the church is the household and family of God. Please join in the call to celebrate.

One: How lovely is your dwelling place, O Lord of hosts!

All: My soul longs, indeed it faints, for the courts of the Lord;

my heart and my flesh sing for joy to the living God (Ps. 84).

One: See what love God has given us, that we should be called children of God;

All: and that is what we are. (1 Jn. 3:1)

One: Come, children of God, let us worship the living Lord!

Invocation

Gracious God, you have chosen to create us in your image and call us your children. We have responded this morning by coming to this house of worship. You have called us together as this household of faith. We recognize that not all households are perfect. Some of us have come with confident faith. But some of us are unsure of our faith and unsure of our part in this household, this family. Some of us have come with questions we are not even sure that we dare ask. We have come, O God, to worship you. Tear down the walls that we construct to hide from you and from one another. Build us into a strong, loving household of faith. Loving God, may our worship be acceptable to you. Amen.

Hymns of Praise

"God of the Earth, the Sky, the Sea" (Longfellow/Hemy) or "Praise the Lord" (Hanaoka)

Hymn of Confession

"Where Charity and Love Prevail" (*Whole Booke of Psalms,* 1592)

Prayer of Confession

One: Loving God, you have created us in your image, adopted us as your children, and called us into this household of faith. We come before you to ask your forgiveness. Forgive us we pray:

People (right side**):** where we have not been a household of compassion, patience, and forgiveness;

People (left side**):** where we have been unwilling to share sorrows and celebrate joys;

People (*right side*): where we have not offered love or been a sister or brother to each other;

People (*left side*): where we have seen only the faults of others and are eager to condemn.

One: Forgive us when, as a community of faith, we have been unwelcoming to the stranger in our midst. Forgive us for when we have called you Creator while we ignored others created in your image. These confessions and our unspoken prayers we offer now to you.

Silent Reflection

Assurance of Pardon

One: Hear the good news. We are God's forgiven household, forgiven to live in right relationship with God and with others. Accept God's forgiveness and receive the power to forgive and to love.

Time with the Children

Bring five small dollhouses and dolls or cardboard cut-out dolls to represent adults and children. Say something like:

> This is the house where Monica lives. She lives with her Grandma and Grandpa. [*Put figures at the house.*] Only the three of them live here. Some households or families have more people.

Ask a child to put the people in front of this house for her or his family. Have a number of children put the correct representation of their household in place. Try to include as many configurations as possible so that every child present is represented. If a child comments that a parent is dead, do not dwell on this but do not ignore it either. It is appropriate to say something like:

> Yes, I remember your mother well. I loved to hear her sing in the choir. So now your family is you and your brother and your Dad.

Continue by saying something like:

> What are some ways we help each other as members of a family?

Help them with suggestions such as love each other, do chores, have fun together, comfort each other in sad times. Try to bring out what it means to be a family.

> The church is our family too. How do we help each other in our church family?

Help them by suggesting teachers teach us, we help newcomers in class by welcoming and showing them where things are.

> Today we are celebrating. We are happy that we belong to this church family. We remember that God loves each one of us. God loves this church family.

Children's Hymn

"There's a Quiet Understanding" (Smith)

Scripture

Ephesians 1:3-6; Mark 3:31-35; 2 Timothy 3:10, 14-15; Colossians 3:12-17

Message

On Being the Household of Faith

Arrange for four people from the congregation to speak for four or five minutes each. Give each person a scripture, the Bible background for that scripture, and one of the following assignments:

a. Like Timothy, each of us has been influenced by models or spiritual heroes. Tell of people who have influenced your spiritual journey. Give specific instances and examples.

b. Tell about your upbringing in another denomination. What family qualities attracted you to *this* church?

c. As a youth, tell about celebrations in your family and in the church. What are your hopes and visions for the family of faith?

d. As a senior member of the church, tell how the church has been a family, for better or worse, over the long haul.

Talk about the trends in the family of faith and impart any advice you have for the church.

Hymn of Response

"Help Us to Help Each Other" (Wesley/Barthelemon)

Family Centres

Give clear instructions for getting to the centres, and announce the time when everyone should return to the congregational celebration. Each person will have time for only one centre.

1. Brothers and Sisters. With the help of a Bible story, this group of youth and adults will have fun getting to know each other. Put chairs in two concentric circles with the same number of chairs inside as outside. Place the chairs on the inside circle so they are facing the chairs in the outside circle. To warm up ask each pair of people facing each other to answer the following questions. After each question, instruct one circle to move several chairs to the left so that everyone will talk with several people.

a. What is your favourite food? What food do you dislike? (Allow 1 minute.)

b. What is your favourite television show? (Allow 90 seconds.)

c. What is your hobby? (Allow 1 minute.)

d. What changes would you like to see in this congregation, this household of faith? (Allow 4 minutes.)

Divide the larger group into four small groups. Assign each group one of the following names: Esau, Jacob, Isaac, and Rebecca. Have a good storyteller briefly tell the main points of the story of Jacob and Esau and their family from Genesis 25:29-34 and Genesis 27:1-45. Instruct the groups to listen to the story from the viewpoint of the person whose name their group was assigned, trying to understand how their character felt.

After the story, have each group list feelings they detected in their character at various points in the story, write the responses on large sheets of newsprint, and post them for the other groups to see. After summarizing their lists, com-pare the feelings of the four characters. Were there any places where more than one character had the same feeling?

Make up four new groups by birthdates. Ask groups to talk about what they liked about the story and what they did not like about it. How did the actions of the grandparents affect the next generation? Can we prevent the mistakes of one generation from adversely influencing the next generation? Do all families have conflicts? Do church families have conflicts? If so, how should they be resolved?

Ask someone from each group to summarize their insights for the whole group.

2. Working Together. Give everyone a marble and ask people to get into groups of six. At one end of the room, have each group form a small circle and place their six marbles in the centre of the circle. Each group's task is to get its marbles to a designated spot at the other end of the room without using their hands. Everyone must participate and the circle formation must not be broken. The marbles must be kept within the circle. You may wish to give a humorous award to the first group who makes it to the other end of the room.

Repeat this exercise, but tell three people in each group that they must remain part of the circle but they cannot help. Afterward make one large circle and discuss the following questions.

a. How did you feel when you were all cooperating?

b. How did you feel when you could not play but were in the circle?

c. How did you feel toward those in your circle who did not help? Did you wish they had opted out of the circle and let the rest of you get the job done?

d. Think of a situation at home, at school, or at work in which you felt like an outsider. Share your experience.

e. Think of another situation when others did not help in the effort. It may be a work situation, a community fundraising project, or a school project.

Share your experience. How did you feel toward those who did not help?

f. Have you ever felt like an outsider in church? Share this situation. How do we make others feel like outsiders? How can we make everyone feel included? Consider situations for all ages. What can we do today and next Sunday and next week to help someone else feel included?

3. The Healing Family. A pastor or qualified deacon or elder should lead this potentially sensitive activity for older youth and adults. If more than eight people participate, divide into smaller groups with one leader in each. Have the participants sit in a circle. The leader will begin by asking for agreement that whatever is shared in this room today is not to be shared outside the room. When confidentiality is assured, people will be more likely to share. Begin by suggesting that all families have some points of friction and hurts; the church family is no exception. Assure them that no one needs to disclose details they prefer not to disclose. Spend a few moments in silent prayer.

When trust has been established and people feel comfortable, sing together "Healer of Our Every Ill" (Haugen) or another hymn of healing.

Now invite those who wish to speak to say what type of healing they seek. Have each one tell her or his story without interruption, unless the leader needs to provide encouragement. Their story could be anything from a single statement such as "I want my broken leg to heal" to a description of a long-standing emotional hurt. The leader will need to be adept at discerning when disclosure needs to be curtailed as well as when pastoral care needs to be given. When each person has told her or his story, invite them individually to be in the centre of the circle for a prayer for healing. The rest of the group may place their hand on the shoulder of the person in the centre during the prayer.

Closing

After reminding the group of confidentiality and assuring them of God's healing power, close by singing "Help Us to Help Each Other" (Wesley/Barthelemon).

4. Created in God's Image. Having been created in the image of God, Christians must take seriously their responsibility to shepherd others in the faith. To begin the session, say to the youth and adults:

> Let us make humankind in our image, according to our likeness" (Gen. 1). *Paul writes at Corinth: "Are you not my work in the Lord?" (1 Cor. 9). These people are Christians because Paul has taught them and been their example. One of the responsibilities God has given us is to teach and influence others. As the family of God, we influence other family members in the same way a parent influences children.*

You may want to add other scriptures that indicate we are God's co-workers.

At least two weeks ahead, ask two people to prepare a simple skit from the following information.

A teacher has a student stay after school because of misconduct. At last the teacher says the child may go home. Instead of moving to go home, the child offers to clean the board and do other chores. Finally the child admits he is not really anxious to go home. The teacher asks why. The child reveals that his parent is an alcoholic and there is abuse in the home.

After the skit say:

> As God's agents, each of us is responsible to help make humankind in our image. Who were the positive "shapers" in your own life? Parents? Siblings? Teachers? Who are your heroes of faith? How can we as Christians in this family, this household, be more intentional about being good role models? as individuals? as a congregation? Should we have a mentor program in our congregation? Do we have a responsibility to take the initiative when we see that there is abuse or lack of

good modelling in the home of someone in our congregation? What, if anything can we do?

5. The Family That Plays Together.

Parents, grandparents, aunts, uncles, adult friends, and young children will have fun playing together. Have the adults teach the children string games and other simple games that they played as children. Then have the children teach the adults games that they play. Talk about the best way to teach—modelling? telling? How do we learn from each other in the church? How can we improve our learning from each other? When have you learned from the children? Give examples. Do you think Jesus learned from others? Give examples. Use building blocks to build a church together.

6. Put Out the Welcome Mat.

Youth and adults will look at the physical plant of the church as well as its organizational structure. Ask the group to imagine that they are newcomers to the community. Walk outside with the group and ask them to look at the church as a potential "home" for their family. What do they see that would invite them to come to this church? Is there a sign indicating what the building is? Is there a way to get into the building if a person is disabled? Now move inside. Is there any indication of when the services take place? If they had never been to a Christian worship service, would this place seem inviting? As they enter, would they feel welcome? Do they know where to go? where the services take place? where the washrooms are? Are there folders or brochures telling about this congregation? On Sunday morning, do the greeters merely say "Good morning" or do they visit with the newcomers? Do the greeters and the ushers help the visitor to feel at home?

Have group members discuss times when they have been visitors. Discuss what has been welcoming and what has not been welcoming. Ask:

> If you are a visitor, do you like to be asked to stand in the service and introduce yourself, or do you find that very embarrassing? *When you have been a visitor, have you found the order of service and the customs of the congregation "strange" and confusing? Do you wish the bulletin would indicate such things as when to stand, which hymnbook to use, how long the service will be? Ask yourselves how we as a congregation and as individuals can make this congregation more welcoming. Do we really want "outsiders" to be a part of this congregation?*

7. Create "Family" Rituals and Customs.

This group of youth and adults will discuss the customs (the written and unwritten rules) of the congregation and changes (if any) that they would like to see. Introduce the topic by saying:

> All families have customs or celebrations, such as ways of commemorating birthdays and holidays. What are some of the traditions in your family? How do these celebrations strengthen *the family? Now think about the customs in this congregation. Which ones are helpful? Where should other traditions be added? Now look at the unwritten rules that make outsiders feel left out. Name a few from your own experience.*

If people need suggestions to get started, talk about the fact that in some congregations only persons X and Z bring apple pie to potlucks, that only homemade pickles are acceptable, that singles can bring only the coffee or tea, that certain pews are reserved for certain people. Then say:

> Think about how tables are set up at church dinners. Are there even numbers of chairs at each t*able that seem to say it is not acceptable to be single? If you are a single mother with several small children, would you like someone sitting near you to offer to help with your children? At congregational meetings, are there unwritten rules about who speaks or is dissent forbidden, for example? In the*

worship service, are there unwritten rules about when to stand and when to sit? How does this make an outsider feel? Are dress customs a difficulty? Are there unwritten rules that only people of a certain sex or age can do certain things? What rules, written or unwritten, make you feel uncomfortable? How is change in the church like change in a family?

8. Make Music Together. This group will sing and play music together. Music helps to unite us as families and as church households. Music is especially important at the significant moments of our lives. Ask the group to list these. Your list will read something like this: birth of a child, dedication of children and parents, birthdays, first day of school, graduating from elementary school, graduating from high school, leaving home for college or first job, baptism, engagement, marriage, wedding anniversary, funeral, Christmas, Epiphany, Easter, Pentecost.

Now start at the beginning of your list, and sing your way through these special occasions. Ask the group to suggest hymns and songs that have been significant at these times. Have lots of different types of music available. Include songs for children and use rhythm instruments for some of them. Discuss ways that the congregation can use music more effectively in making everyone feel more included.

Gathering Again

As the congregation reassembles, have someone with a guitar play the hymn "Will You Let Me Be Your Servant" (Gillard), on page 78. When everyone is present, a soloist will sing the hymn as two dancers interpret it. If the congregation knows the hymn, divide the congregation in half with each half turning to face the other, and invite them to sing to each other: "Will you let me be your servant, let me be as Christ to you?"

Affirmation of Faith

One: We believe that we have been created in the image of God.

All: We believe that we are God's co-workers, called to be as Christ to others.

We believe that we have been called to this household of faith to encourage one another to grow in faith, to proclaim forgiveness and healing and reconciliation, to bear witness to the power of light over darkness, to announce the good news.

We believe that the good news is for all peoples.

We believe that we are no longer foreigners but citizens with God's people and members of the household of God, living stones with Christ as the chief cornerstone of our church household. Thanks be to God.

Pastoral Prayer

Incorporate prayer concerns for members of the church family and the global family.

Offering

Hymn of Commission

"For Christ and the Church" (Hewitt/Kirkpatrick). The banner is carried out during this hymn and placed in the fellowship hall where it can be seen during the meal.

Benediction

Family Reunion

The ushers will hand each person (except very young children who need to stay with a parent or adult) a slip of paper from a basket as they leave the worship. These papers will have a number from 1 to 10 (depending on the size of your congregation) for the person's table assignment. The tables in the fellowship hall will be set up for ten people each and covered with paper tablecloths. Each table will be given a number. Place ten or twelve crayons on each table.

Ahead of time organize a potluck meal with drinks and dessert provided. Have extra food on hand for visitors and those who may have forgotten to bring their sack lunches. People will go to the table with their number on it to find their "family." This family will say grace together, serve each other, eat together, and tell family stories over the meal. Appoint a host ahead of time to lead the family through the questions below. Leaders should take care to let everyone contribute a story for each question.

a. What is your saddest memory in the church?

b. What is your happiest or funniest memory in the church?

c. Who are your church heroes?

d. What is your favourite church tradition? Christmas? Camp? Bible study? Other?

e. Together say the books of the Bible in order without looking.

f. On your placemats or paper tablecloths, draw portraits of the first Sunday school teacher you can remember.

g. Make wishes for the church family.

Closing Hymn

"Blest Be the Tie That Binds" (Fawcett/Nägeli)

Your finished house
should look like this

Will You Let Me Be Your Servant?

1,6 Will you let me be your servant, let me
2 We are pil - grims on a jour - ney, we are
3 I will hold the Christ - light for you in the
4 I will weep when you are weep - ing, when you
5 When we sing to God in heav - en, we shall

1,6 be as Christ to you? Pray that I may have the
2 trav - 'lers on the road. We are here to help each
3 night - time of your fear. I will hold my hand out
4 laugh I'll laugh with you. I will share your joy and
5 find such har - mo - ny, born of all we've known to -

1,6 grace to let you be my ser - vant too.
2 oth - er walk the mile and bear the load.
3 to you, speak the peace you long to hear.
4 sor - row till we've seen this jour - ney through.
5 geth - er of Christ's love and a - gon - y.

*Guitar chords for unison singing only

Text: Richard Gillard, 1977, alt.
Music: Richard Gillard, 1977; adapted by Betty Pulkingham
Text and Music copyright © 1977 Scripture in Song
(Administered by Maranatha Music, c/o The Copyright Company, Nashville, TN)
All rights reserved. International copyright secured. Used by permission.

Christ Has Broken Down the Dividing Walls

Celebrate Cultures

I truly understand that God shows no partiality, but in every nation anyone who fears God and does what is right is acceptable to God.

—Acts 10:34

Most of us, if asked to make a self-evaluation, would probably rate ourselves as hospitable people who do justice and show love. Most of us would say that we hold no racial prejudice. In the 1960s, the movie *Guess Who's Coming to Dinner* challenged many people to examine how they would respond if their beliefs on race and culture were put to the test. The story is about a white newspaper editor who had often criticized racial intolerance in his paper, but only faced his own prejudice when his beloved daughter invited a black man home for dinner. Those who saw the film were forced to grapple with the issue of table fellowship. The way we respond to this issue reflects, interestingly, as much about how we view ourselves as about how we view others.

Our tendency to view ourselves as superior to others seems to be a human weakness. Isaiah tried to heal this disease. Paul had to deal with it too. Author H.G. Wells wrote: "There is no more evil thing in this present world than race prejudice, none at all! It is the worst single thing in life. It justifies and holds together more obscene cruelty and abomination than any other sort of error in the world." We do not have to look farther than our own neighbourhoods to see the truth of this statement.

Celebrating cultures helps us see the alternative to prejudice that the scriptures offer. The exciting truth is that Jesus and other early church leaders viewed the racial and ethnic differences not as problems to be solved or obstacles to be overcome, but a blessing to be enjoyed and celebrated, a blessing that honours God and enriches our worship.

Bible Text

Isaiah 55–56; Galatians 3; Acts 8; 10; 11; Ruth

Bible Background for Our Celebration

The poet in Isaiah uses the metaphor of a banquet to represent God's unconditional love for all who wish to come. Food and drink are life-giving and freely given by God no matter what a person looks like or what culture he or she belongs to. When Isaiah said "Ho, everyone who thirsts . . . ," he is proclaiming that God's love is inclusive.

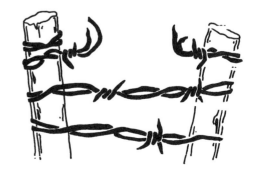

Several times in ancient Hebrew life, the people of God faced annihilation. One of those periods was the time they were conquered by the Babylonians and marched off to captivity in Babylon. The other was in the time of Jesus and Paul when the Jews lived under Roman occupation. In both cases, the people of God had the impulse to preserve their faith and culture by forbidding any but the racially and ethnically pure to be part of their community.

Isaiah, however, compared faith to a banquet—all who hunger and thirst may eat. It is not just the Hebrews who eat. Anyone who has a spiritual hunger, which includes people of all nations and races, may "eat" at God's table. Isaiah directed his teaching at the Hebrews who tried to exclude brothers and sisters in exile who had mixed with the local culture and taken on some of the practices of Babylonian religion in addition to their own monotheism. The Hebrews also spurned their brothers and sisters in the homeland who strayed from the law and mingled with the local religions and cultures.

The prophet also invites the poor to be part of God's people: "He who has no money, come." The banquet is for rich and poor alike. The criterion for those to be included has nothing to do with worthiness. Those with or without wealth may eat. What is required is the hunger for the word. And everyone hun-gers. The prophet insisted that to share fully in fellowship with God's worshipers requires only loyalty to the covenant, which results in the outward expression of faithful living.

Paul had to address the same lack of inclusiveness many generations later. In his letter to the Galatians, Paul argues for inclusiveness. He knows that the good news of God's grace brings a unity not founded on ethnic heritage. Paul does not say, however, that the distinctions will disappear; rather he says that we are to view them from a new perspective. As Bible scholar Charles Cousar writes:

> [Differences between people do not vanish;] . . . the barriers, the hostility, the chauvinism, and the sense of superiority and inferiority between respective categories are destroyed. Being in Christ does not do away with Jew or Greek, male or female . . . but it makes these differences before God irrelevant.

Faith Nugget

As followers of Christ, we define our fellowship by hunger, not by skin colour or culture.

Early Preparation

1. Four to six weeks before the service, recruit the storyteller who will be presenting the message and give her the script.

2. Invite the five people who will be the group discussion leaders.

3. Ask the four storytellers to prepare the story for each centre or have these stories put on tape.

4. Prepare the well. Use gray mural paper on which stones have been drawn to represent the outside of the well. Cardboard from boxes may be used to build the well. A few real stones may be placed around the edge. OR if someone in your congregation has an ornamental wishing well on their front lawn, remove the top and use that. In either case, for the discussion time, you will need a tub or at least a pail into which water can be poured.

5. Prepare tags for each person who comes to worship. These tags will be numbered from one to five to indicate which group the person will join.

6. Collect dolls and other items to represent many different countries.

7. Give the music information to the musicians.

8. Arrange for a committee to prepare an ethnic fellowship meal.

You will need
- ❑ bulletins for the participants
- ❑ cardboard well
- ❑ bucket of water
- ❑ dolls or souvenirs from around the world
- ❑ an international cookbook: *Extending the Table*

Name of your church
Christ Has Broken Down the Dividing Walls
Celebrate Cultures

Call To Worship

Invocation

Hymns of Praise . . . . "Let the Whole Creation Cry" "From All That Dwell Below the Sky"

Prayer of Confession

Silent Confession

Assurance of Pardon

Scripture. . . . . Isaiah 55:1,5; 56:3-8; Galatians 3:26-29

Message. . . . . "A Mirror at the Bottom of the Cup"

Hymn of Response. . . . . "For We Are Strangers No More"

Culture Centres:
1. Drawing from the Well. We put ourselves in the place of the woman at the well.
2. Essentials. Meet Peter who learned about acceptance in a dream.
3. The Immigrant. Ruth takes the risk of living in a foreign culture.
4. Closed Doors. The Ethiopian finds a closed door and an open door.
5. Two Gutsy Women. Despite custom, Mary and Martha are true disciples of Jesus.

Gathering Hymns

Pastoral Prayer

Offering

Hymn of Commission . . . . "Filled with the Spirit's Power"

Benediction

Fellowship Meal

The Celebration

As people enter, give each one a small piece of paper with a number from 1 to 5 on it. This number will tell a person at which centre to begin. Try to keep the groups of equal size.

At the centre of your worship area rig up a well. Make it of cardboard painted to look like stone, or borrow a decorative wishing well from someone in the congregation. In the centre of the well, conceal a five-gallon bucket of water.

On a table near the well, display a collection of dolls from around the world or a collection of souvenirs from various countries. Let them represent the variety of cultures in which Christians live.

Call to Worship

Ho, everyone who thirsts, come to the waters;

Seek the Lord, and call upon God's name.

God is the Creator and Redeemer and Lover of all the peoples of the world.

Come, let us worship and offer our praise to God.

Invocation

God of all creation, God of all peoples, Loving Parent, we have come to worship you. May the words of our mouths and the meditations of our hearts be acceptable to you, we pray. Make yourself known to us as we come before you with open hearts and minds. May we allow the fresh breeze of your Spirit to sweep out all that is unworthy and to fill us with new wisdom, inspired insights, and inclusive love. Amen.

Hymns of Praise

"Let The Whole Creation Cry" (Brooke/ Williams) and "From All That Dwell Below the Sky" (Hatton) or other hymns of praise

Prayer of Confession

Creator and Preserver of all humanity, we have called you Father and Mother and Parent, but we have failed to see that all peoples are our sisters and brothers. We confess that we have allowed the prejudices of our culture to blind us to the pain others suffer because of injustice. We confess where we have not spoken out for people who have been confined and restricted by stereotypes imposed by society. We confess that we have misused your scriptures to suppress the freedom of others. Forgive us we pray.

Silent Confession

Assurance of Pardon

Sisters and brothers, hear the good news: God is a gracious God and rich in mercy. God is faithful and just to forgive us our sins and will renew a right spirit within us. Thanks be to God.

Scripture

Introduce the scriptures by reading the following:

For most of us it is difficult to comprehend just how radical the actions of Jesus were when he broke the cultural norms of his time. We find it hard to imagine walking all the way around a country, as Jews did around Samaria, just to avoid encountering foreigners. We find it difficult to put ourselves in the shoes of a man who, like the Jewish men of Jesus' day, could not talk to a woman in public, not even his own mother. But we have our own modern equivalents of unconscious discrimination.

Many of us skirt "bad" sections of town or stereotype whole groups of people as being unambitious, satisfied with their poverty, and amoral. We wouldn't refuse to speak to anyone, but we are so geared to living in a man's world or a woman's world, we don't always know how to speak to one another and end up leaving someone out.

When it comes to foreigners, we offend easily because we don't know much about other cultures. For instance, it is an insult to an Arab if you expose the filthy sole of your shoe as you sit with legs crossed, a very common posture in western culture. On the other hand, non-Arabs might take offense at the Arab practice of greeting with a kiss. There are many ways we misunderstand each other.

A minister came face-to-face with cultural traditions that challenged his convictions. About thirty-five of the parishioners in his church were Korean. After church these families often met at one of their homes and had a meal together. The minister was sometimes invited. He discovered that the men sat in the living room. The children were in another room. The women met in the kitchen and came to the living room only to serve the meal to the men. In an attempt to be Christlike, the minister went to the kitchen to offer to help, but he was met by an older woman who invited him to remain with the men. For him to help to prepare the meal or to do the dishes was improper in her experience. His dilemma: How could he be faithful and yet not offend? By learning a little more of their culture he found his answer. He went to the room where the children were, picked up a tiny child, and carried the child to the kitchen. In Korean culture a man with a child becomes an honorary woman. Now he could enter the kitchen and help.

Read Isaiah 55:1,5; Isaiah 56:3-8; Galatians 3:26-29.

Message

"A Mirror at the Bottom of the Cup" (see Resources for this Celebration)

Hymn of Response

"For We Are Strangers No More" (Morse/Morningstar) or "In Christ There Is No East or West" or other hymn of inclusiveness

Culture Centres

Instead of choosing one activity, people will circulate to each of five stations. They will go first to the station designated by the number on the slip of paper they received at the beginning of the celebration. After fifteen minutes in a centre, they will move on to the other four in numerical order. Group one will remain in the worship centre around the well. See the resource section for instructions for each centre.

Gathering Hymns

When everyone has visited each of the five centres, gather again in the worship area for the last part of the celebration. As people are making their way back, sing hymns about Jesus' love for all, such as:

"Jesus Loves the Little Children" (Woolston/ Root)

"Long Ago When Jesus" (Bayly/Finlay)

"When I Needed a Neighbor" (Carter)

"Here in This Place" (Haugen)

If there are people whose first language is not English, include a hymn in their language.

Pastoral Prayer

Offering

Different countries have different money. Some of it depicts heroes, founders, landmarks, and historic sites. It is colourful and sometimes very beautiful. The thing that all money has in common, though, is that it has value. God's people are the same. Regardless of variety, colour, or image, God's people have value. Let us be generous in giving away this money that we value so highly, and let us be generous in the value we place on our brothers and sisters in Christ.

The choir sings as the offering is brought forward: "Creating God, Your Fingers Trace" (Rowthorn/Clemens).

Hymn of Commission

"Filled with the Spirit's Power" or other sending hymn

Benediction

"What God has made clean, you must not call profane" (Acts 10:15). If you hunger and thirst for righteousness, go to the banquet and eat with your brothers and sisters. Amen.

Fellowship Meal

Prepare a fellowship meal with dishes representing the various ethnic groups in your denomination or congregation. See *Extending the Table*, an international cookbook with meditations from Christians around the world (available from Herald Press).

A Mirror at the Bottom of the Cup: the Way It Might Have Been

Setting:
A woman, in costume suggesting she is a first-century Samaritan, tells the story. The story is most effectively told from memory. Her only props are a water jug and a long, lightweight scarf. In the monologue, she removes the scarf from her neck, twists it tightly, winds it into the shape of a doughnut, and places it on her head. It is on this that the water jug is set.

[*The Samaritan woman enters from the side and makes her way slowly to the well.*]

People still ask me about that day. It was a day I'll never forget. It was hot and sticky. And I was out of water—again. I almost decided not to go for water. I'd had enough of the whispers and gossip behind my back from other women who think they're too good to speak to me. Humph. Or is it that their husbands are afraid I will give their wives ideas? That's probably it.

[*She begins twisting and winding the scarf.*]

That day I picked up my water jar and started out. Along the way I would catch my neighbours peeking out from behind the curtains; I wanted to say to them: Yes, I am with a new man. What choices do I have? That arranged marriage when I was fourteen . . . well the old man wanted a slave, not a wife.

[*With the pail on her head, she moves to the well and ties a rope to the bail on the bucket.*]

[*Getting serious*] I was a person of strong opinions. And I was naive. Yes, very naive. But I was smart enough to know what it meant when I saw my shoes outside the door that day. I was being thrown out.
I learned quickly what it meant to be divorced. I also learned that I was a

failure at fifteen, according to others anyway. I was a disgrace to the family, a burden. What could I do? I was considered used goods. All the things they said about me I began to believe. Then I proved them right. I let any man who came along grab me for his own property.

After my husband divorced me, I used to sit against the outer wall. It was a place of protection. A place to rest. A place to sleep and a place to pretend to sleep. You'd be surprised what I learned sitting there. I heard the rabbis teaching their followers, and I heard them pray. [*Mimicking the rabbi, she says.*] "Thank you, God, that I was not born a woman." Bah! Why is it a sin to be born a woman? I finally got that one figured out. Well anyway, I also learned composition and disposition and exhortation and exposition. Probably it was exposition [*lifts skirt slightly, coyly*] that kept me from starving.

I got up to finish my walk to the well. Look at that, would you, I said to myself. A rabbi. A Jewish rabbi, at a Samaritan well no less. Now I've seen everything. How often have I heard the Jewish saying: "It is better to eat the flesh of swine than to eat Samaritan bread." Well, if he thinks I'm turning back, he's got another think coming! It's our well. What's he doing in Samaria anyway?

The Palestinian Jews always walk all around our little country. Silly arrogance. Afraid they'll be contaminated. Maybe it's just a case of sore feet. So he will pretend that I am not there, and I will get my water and ignore him.

At the well I got ready to draw my water. "Would you give me a drink?" he asked. I looked up sharply. Who was he talking to? Certainly not to me, I thought, but no one else was there.

"Pardon me?"

"Would you give me a drink ?" he asked.

What is this? A Jew from Galilee talking to a Samaritan? Impossible. A Jewish rabbi talking to a woman in public. Preposterous. I have seen those rabbis cross the street when they saw their own mother coming so they would not have to speak to a woman in public. What trick is he trying to play on me? Was this a trap?

Then we began to match verbal wits. We threw puns back and forth like children splashing water on each other. His conversation was serious. He was not out to entrap me. He treated me as an equal. I tested him by seeing what would happen if I engaged him in conversation about religion. We had the most unbelievable talk. I thought of all those rabbinical sayings like "It is better to teach your daughter lasciviousness than to teach her the law." I thought of all the taboos he was breaking, all the barriers that he had removed just to talk to me, a foreigner and a woman.

He took the cup of water and offered it to me. Reluctantly, hesitatingly, I took it. When I drank I could see my reflection at the bottom of the cup. This rabbi was holding a mirror up to my innermost self. He took me on an inward journey past the stereotypes, past the years of oppression, past the experiences of devaluation, until I discovered something within that I never would have believed could be there. He took me to a place of healing. A place where I

experienced a sense of my own sacredness. Me. Made in the image of God. Me. He revealed that inside me there is a spring of living water, an unfailing source of the gift of the spirit. Inside me! It was as though I was reborn.

"Who are you?" I asked. "You must be the Messiah."

"I am," he said.

"But why haven't I heard of you before?"

"Because you are the first person to whom I have publicly revealed this." To me. To me a Samaritan woman. A much married Samaritan woman!

"Go back to the village," he said. "Go back and tell them."

[*She begins to speak very fast.*]

I left my water jug. I ran back to the village. I could not contain my good news. The words just spilled out. I discovered that the people were thirsting, parched for the living water. There they were, standing by the old wells hoping to draw water from the ancient traditions. There they were, longing to discover their own hidden wells. There they were, yearning to meet God within. There they were, underneath all that composure and self-righteousness and respectability; there they were, searching for healing and wisdom and strength. There they were, just like me, dreaming of wellsprings of new vision and hope and shalom and world community.

[*Pausing and then speaking slowly*]

Suddenly I realized that all these people were listening to me. To me. In that spring of living water within me there was power!

"Go," I said at last, "See for yourself." I needed time to be alone. I needed time to reflect. I needed time to think and to ponder. I have been pondering and wondering and . . . living . . . ever since. I marvelled how Jesus had called me from the outer fringe, the margin of life, to the centre of life, and empowered me to be the bearer of revelation to my community. If he called me, surely he has called you. [*Winds the scarf and places it on her head. Then she puts the pail on her head.*]

I saw that in order to drink from our own wells we must be willing to courageously look beyond the established beliefs and culture and traditions. We must look at who God says we are, not what society and culture say we are.

For whom can you hold the mirror?

Whom would you ask to "Give me a drink"?

What ancient barriers are you called to remove?

To whom will you offer a cup of water?

Culture Centres

You will need five locations plus the worship area. Station a discussion leader in each area. You will also need five excellent storytellers, one to tell the Message story and four for the culture centres. If you do not have superb storytellers, have one or two people put the stories on tape.

The storytellers and discussion leaders will remain at their centres, and the participants will rotate. You will need a signal to mark the end of each period of twelve to fifteen minutes each. Number the centres 1-5, with the worship centre as Centre 1.

Centre 1 (worship centre).
A Mirror at the Bottom of the Cup

This group meets in the worship area around the well. This is the only centre in which a story will not be told. It will focus instead on the story that has been told in the message, and the person who portrayed the woman at the well will be present. The discussion leader may want to ask her about her feelings.

Each person, including the discussion leader, is given a small pail of water and a small cup (a punch cup or scoop or paper cup) for dipping. Put a large tub of water in the centre of the well to hold the contents of the smaller pails. Then divide the group randomly into four sub-groups. Label these smaller groups as follows: Jesus' disciples, the Samaritan woman, the townspeople who looked out from behind the curtains and who lived near the woman, and the Jews who avoided walking through Samaria.

The discussion leader explains that the pail of water represents the positive feelings we each start out with. Each time someone insults us or in some way hurts us we lose some of our feeling of worth. The leader gives everyone a full pail of water and begins reading a list of questions. If participants believe they have lost some feeling of self-worth, they must put a cupful back into the well. Also, the person who made us feel bad loses and that person too must put a cupful into the well.

Here are some of the kinds of questions the discussion leader will use to initiate the discussion.

To the Disciples: You have been accustomed to walking around Samaria. How do you feel when Jesus says that today you will be walking through Samaria? What are some of the things you say to each other out of earshot of Jesus? What are your thoughts about Samaritans? What are some of your feelings when you see Jesus talking with the woman?

To the Samaritans: What thoughts go through your mind when you see the Jews avoiding your country? What did you feel when you saw Jesus and the disciples enter Samaria? What was your reaction when you saw him visit with the woman at the well? How did you feel toward this woman?

To the Jews who avoided Samaria: When you were learning the ancient sayings, did you think God included all people or just some people in the family of God? Did you consider the Samaritans as fellow-Jews? What were your feelings as you skirted the Samaria area?

To the woman: How did you feel when Jesus talked to you as an equal? How did you feel when Jesus told you that you, a Samaritan and a woman, were the first to whom he publicly revealed his mission? How did you feel when you were given the mission to tell the good news? Did the people believe you?

To the group as a whole: Has anyone ever despised you because of your ethnic origin? Tell about it. Have you ever been prejudiced? Tell about one of your prejudices. What can the congregation do to be more inclusive and reach out to all people?

Centre 2.
The Man Who Came to Dinner and Rewrote the Guest List (Acts 10)

Imagine die-hard vegetarians and loyal meat eaters having dinner together! In this story, not only do the dietary customs of the guests differ, the religions, nationalities, occupations, and social status of the two guests are far apart. How did these two ever get together? It was nothing short of a miracle.

One of the dinner partners was Cornelius, the captain of a Roman legion. He commanded anywhere from 300 to 600 men in the Roman army that occupied Palestine in Paul's time. Now Cornelius was a moral man and a religious man. He realized the emptiness of paganism and had searched for a deeper spirituality. In his search, he discovered the one God, the God of the Jews. Or more accurately, God sought him out and responded to Cornelius's prayers.

The other dinner partner was a Jewish fisherman from the other side of town. Peter (nicknamed "the Rock") had never been an overly zealous Jew, but he certainly knew enough to stick firmly to the dietary laws and to his own kind and not to mix it up with "those Gentiles." Even after being with Jesus and having his eyes opened about what God was all about, Peter would never go as far as to minister to the Gentiles. After all, he'd had a lifetime of indoctrination about those foreigners and like most rocks he was pretty set in his ways.

It was about three o'clock in the afternoon, in broad daylight, when it happened. Cornelius was on coffee break and was using the time, as he often did, to spend time in prayer to God. Suddenly it was as though an angel were standing right there and speaking to him. "Cornelius."

"What is it, Lord?" he asked, not mentioning that he was too scared to say anything more.

"God has a job for you. Send two or three of your men to Joppa. Tell them to go to the house of Simon the Tanner and ask for Peter. Have your men bring Peter to your house."

Cornelius was a man accustomed to giving orders. He expected his orders to be obeyed immediately, so that is how he responded: he immediately sent his men to Joppa.

Now it so happened that as these men were en route to Joppa, Peter the Rock was at the home of Simon the Tanner, sitting on the rooftop to cool off. It was right there that God came to Peter, not in the temple or holy place, but in a very ordinary place. In that ordinary place God sent an extraordinary, spine-tingling vision to Peter while he was in prayer. In the vision, a large sheet came down by its four corners from heaven. In the sheet were all kinds of animals, animals that Peter was accustomed to eating and those that no good Jew would ever consider fit to eat. It was terrifying to see them together, all mixed up like that. But worse, Peter heard God tell him to get up and eat. "Eat, from this mixed bag?" he thought. "Not on your life! I have never eaten anything unclean or impure."

Well, it took God three attempts to finally convince "the Rock" to eat. In spite of all Peter's solid rock beliefs, he received Cornelius's men and accepted their invitation to dine at Cornelius's home. He went to the house of a Gentile, a forbidden place for Jews, and ate.

Cornelius's house was full of people who had come to hear about God. Peter spoke of God's love for all and then stopped to ask who wanted to be baptized. What a baptismal service they had!

On that day the guest list was rewritten. It no longer said: My ethnic group only. From that day on it read: There is only one race: the human race. God welcomes us all.

Discussion

a. Tell about how your convictions have changed.

b. In your opinion, what gives rise to feelings of racial superiority?

c. Which customs in your congregation are a matter of faith and which are matters of tradition and preference? Which would you be willing to change?

d. How do we become an inclusive church and yet have solid beliefs and standards?

Centre 3.
Shaking the Family Tree (Ruth)

Famine is what drove an Israeli family to the land of Moab in the first place. Then when everything seemed to be going well again, the father and the sons died. Alone in the world, Naomi, the mother, longed to return to her homeland and to her relatives.

Naomi took it for granted that her sons' widows would want to remain in Moab with their people, but one of them, Ruth, insisted on coming with her. Naomi tried to dissuade her, though she must have been glad to have her daughter-in-law on the long walk home. And she must have been especially happy when Ruth confided that she was a worshiper of Yahweh and was looking forward to worshiping with Naomi in her homeland.

Not long after they were settled, a farmer named Boaz, the son of Rahab, took a more than passing interest in this young foreigner. He told his hired help to look out for her and make sure that her gathering basket was always well filled, because he had heard that she was very good to her mother-in-law and

that she also was his distant cousin by marriage.

Now, Naomi might be getting older but she certainly was not blind and she was nobody's fool. She called Ruth and gave her courting instructions. After a long hot day in the fields, all of the men would be tired and they would eat a big meal and fall asleep in the barn. Naomi told Ruth to slip into the barn at midnight. About then Boaz might just have his feet sticking out from under the blanket and a nice warm body covering them would feel great.

Ruth did as Naomi had instructed, one thing led to another, and eventually she and Boaz were married. Later they had a child. The honour of naming the child was given to Naomi. She named him Obed. Obed grew up and married and had a son named Jesse. And Jesse had seven sons, the youngest of whom was David. David turned out to be one of, if not the greatest, kings Israel ever had. Perhaps David's descendants, however, did not want to shake the family tree to discover that Rahab and Ruth, a foreigner from Moab, were their ancestors. After all, how could they then claim to be a pure and separate race? Yet, God surely knew what was going on!

Discussion

a. How much did you know about the ancestry of Jesus before you heard this story? Why do you think God chose this ancestry for Jesus?

b. Why do people try to hide the "skeletons" in their genealogical closet?

c. From where did Ruth and Naomi draw strength and courage to confront all of the cultural taboos of their time? Name a modern parallel.

Centre 4.
The Man Who Came to Worship (Acts 8)

He was the minister of finance in the royal government of Ethiopia. He was a man who contemplated the big questions of life. He read widely. He was not a Jew, but he believed in one God as the Jews believed. So he set out to Jerusalem to see what he could learn and experience in the temple at Jerusalem.

In Jerusalem, as he approached the temple, a hand grasped his shoulder. One of the authorities told him he could go no further. As a foreigner and a eunuch, he could not enter the temple to worship. He asked them why it was that he could not worship in the temple and they showed him the scriptures. He read the text from Leviticus: "No one who has a blemish . . . no hunchback, or a dwarf, or a man . . . with an itching disease . . . or crushed testicles" (21:17-21). And besides, they said, no foreigner could worship with them.

There was nothing to do but go home. On his return journey he fell into contemplation. Why, he wondered, was this one God so harsh? Why was this God so exclusive? As he drove along he decided to study the scriptures to look for answers to his question. Suddenly he came upon these startling words from Isaiah: "Do not let the foreigner joined to the Lord say, 'The Lord will surely separate me from his people'; and do not let the eunuch say, 'I am just a dry tree.' " The scripture went on to say that the eunuch and the foreigner were to be welcomed! (Isa. 56:3-8).

As he was driving along reading out loud, a certain disciple of Jesus named Philip was walking along the same road. The disciple asked if he understood what he was reading. What a conversation followed! Philip answered all his questions, told him about Jesus, gave him the whole gospel story.

The minister of finance noticed that they were passing a little pond by the road. He asked what was stopping Philip from baptizing him right there. Philip could not think of any reason to prevent his baptism.

There by the side of the road, Philip baptized and welcomed the minister of finance into the church. This foreigner, this eunuch, was his Christian brother.

Discussion

a. Which scriptures have been used to exclude or ostracize people, such as left-handed people, slaves, and alleged witches?

b. How do you respond when people use selected verses to "prove" that God is exclusive?

c. How do you read the Bible? Do you think the Bible speaks to what is or to what ought to be according to God's will, or both?

d. Who are today's foreigners? Who are today's eunuchs?

Centre 5.
Two Gutsy Women (Luke 10; John 11—12)

Jesus often challenged people to be free. He opened doors for people, but many were not eager to walk through them. Sometimes it requires courage and a tough skin and great faith, like that of the two sisters who were Jesus' friends.

Martha's husband had died. In those days a woman was at the bottom of the pecking order and a woman without a man had no status at all. But Martha could not abide by convention. She bucked every social norm to become a disciple of Jesus. She was encouraged by his teaching that God loved everyone equally, rich and poor, male and female, Gentile and Jew.

Martha realized that as Jesus travelled he needed a place to stay. So Martha invited Jesus to stay in her home in the village of Bethany whenever he came through on his way to Jerusalem. She had made a home for her younger sister Mary and brother Lazarus. Now her home became a gathering place and a retreat for Jesus and his disciples. Mary and Martha and the others could openly discuss matters of faith and belief with Jesus. They became his disciples.

Jesus' teaching opened the eyes of Mary and Martha; they saw the grace and love of God as they had never dared to believe before. They saw Jesus live out this love as he spoke openly with women, lepers, tax collectors, and demon-possessed people. Here was a preacher who publicly was not only willing to engage outcasts in theological conversation, he also broke down the taboos and touched them and healed them. This was a man of God. This was a rabbi who would be sure to feel the wrath of the establishment.

When Mary and Martha's brother, Lazarus, died, Martha spoke forthrightly to Jesus in public, something a woman would not have dared to do. She said, "If you had been here, my brother would not have died. But I know that even now God will give you whatever you ask." Right there on the spot, they discussed the theology of the resurrection.

Six days before the Passover, Martha held a dinner party for Jesus and his disciples. Everyone was tense because of the plots afoot to kill Jesus. The authorities thought he was gaining too many followers and stirring up a revolution. The dinner party was a celebration in honor of Jesus, but it was overshadowed by talk of his death.

As they were reclining at the table, Mary slipped off to her room. There she took from its hiding place her total savings—a pint of pure nard. How long it must have taken her to save this much—a year's wage for a working man, one can only guess. Then, with courage and love, she walked through the door of freedom that Jesus had opened. She broke all of the old taboos about unclean feet and covered head and women eating separately in the kitchen when she broke the vial of perfume and poured it over Jesus feet, anointing him for his death and new life.

Discussion

a. Have you ever experienced discrimination because of cultural customs like the length of your hair, the type of clothes you wear, or the kind of food you eat?

b. Have you ever experienced discrimination or limitation because you were pigeonholed into a certain role, such as young or old, female or male, rich or poor, educated or unschooled, married or single?

c. Have you experienced discrimination because of your language or accent or skin color?

d. Have you been made to feel that your type of worship is not as worthy as another's?

e. How has Christ offered you freedom?

A Celebration of the Early Church

Celebrate Our Christian Heritage

Most people are bothered by those passages of Scripture which they cannot understand; but as for me, I have always noticed that the passages in Scripture which trouble me most are those which I do understand.

—Mark Twain

The church is struggling with many serious issues. There are those who say that these issues will tear the church apart. Some even predict the demise of the established church. When we look back at first-century Christians, we see that they faced an issue that many scholars today believe was of a much more divisive nature than anything we face. And they faced this when the church was still in its birth pangs! Yet the church survived and flourished! Our service today celebrates the enthusiasm of the early church and tries to replicate the encouragement and mutual upbuilding that the persecuted church was able to muster for its sister congregations.

Bible Text

Acts 15:1-2; 1 Corinthians 10:23-31; Matthew 16:13-18; Matthew 13:16-18, 31-33

Bible Background for Our Celebration

It has often been said that Jesus did not establish a church and that the idea of a church was foreign to the mind of Jesus. However, the way Jesus formed a community of believers and used them to carry out the good news became the model for "church" as we know it. The earliest name for the church was simply "the meeting" or "the association." In Acts 2:42, we learn that the followers were constantly together either in the courts of the temple or in private homes, where they engaged in prayer, shared a common meal, and listened to the teaching of the Apostles. At this time they had no official leader, but Peter was the guiding spirit. Later, leaders such as Phoebe and Prisca and Aquila emerged (Rom. 16:1-5). The members were all considered equal and each one could speak freely.

At this time, the church had no fixed creed. The closest they came to a statement of faith or creed was to say "Jesus is Lord," which was used more as a vow of allegiance. It appears that they closed each of their daily meals together by repeating what Jesus had said and done with the disciples at their last meal. This was done to remind them that they were still in fellowship with him.

At first, Christians continued to worship in the synagogues and considered themselves Jews, but the authorities began to view them and their ideas about Jesus as a threat to the faith. Finally, Christians were expelled from the synagogues, and they took with them many of the elements of worship from the synagogue to their new Christian congregations.

Christian worship was not a precise copy of synagogue worship. There was a new emphasis on expressing the new revelation and new spirit. Letters from the Apostles were read and new hymns were composed. Christian worship arose from the fusion of the synagogue and the upper room. Some traditions, such as the Kiddush, were adopted and adapted for Christian worship. In Judaism, it was a simple meal shared weekly by a rabbi and his disciples. In Christianity, it became the Communion meal. This, the Kiddush, was probably the last meal that Jesus and the disciples had together.

Life of the earliest Christians was greatly influenced by the belief that Jesus' return was imminent, perhaps as near as a few days or weeks. When the burgeoning church began to realize that the wait could be very long, it began to organize itself for the long haul.

The growing Christian movement not only threatened the Jewish authorities; the Roman authorities didn't like them much either. For many years Christians worshiped in secret and were persecuted when discovered. Suppression of the church made it necessary for Christians to hide even the dead. Grave diggers became a low rank of clergy and were responsible for digging what are called the catacombs, an extensive sys-

tem of underground tunnels for burial and worship. The entrance to most of the catacombs was near or in a church. The symbols found there do not include a cross. Symbols that have been found include the Greek monogram for Christ, dove, peacock, and pelican. There are paintings of a youthful beardless Shepherd, a woman standing in an attitude of prayer to personify the soul of the departed, depictions of the raising of Lazarus, and depictions of Jesus and the woman at the well. The dove symbolized the Spirit, the peacock was a borrowed symbol for immortality, the pelican represented the Redeemer. (There was a common fable that if a snake bit a young pelican the parent would tear its breast to revive the young with its blood. The peacock was sacred to Juno. A peacock was released at the funeral of an empress to signify her deification.)

As in any human community, disagreements arose in the early Christian community. The most serious disagreement was over whether to require converts to become Jewish first. This issue had the potential for tearing the young church apart. It was not solved quickly or easily or painlessly.

Faith Nugget

The community of believers is entrusted with the mission of Jesus, which is often at odds with the powers of the world.

Early Preparation

1. Locate first-century type lamps for the visual call to worship in each gathering place.

2. Meet with leaders to plan and assign rooms if using the church. Or seek volunteers to offer their homes for meeting away from the church.

3. Make sure that each leader has appropriate materials for each participant.

4. If the celebration takes place in small groups, you will need one set of letters or readings for each group and bulletins and hymnals for all participants. You may choose not to use all five readings.

You will need
- ❑ someone to be the "lookout" at each meeting place
- ❑ sheets of paper and markers

- poster board cut into 2″ squares for each participant
- heavy string or cord
- craft glue
- aluminum foil
- safety pins or jewelry clasps
- a set of readings for each group (in envelopes)
- stamped postcards

Your church name

A Celebration
of the Early Church
Celebrate Our Christian Heritage

Gather in Secret

Make a Sign

Hymn of Gathering . . . . "What Is This Place?"

Call to Worship

Invocation

Hymns of Praise . . . . "Shepherd of Eager Youth"
"O Splendor of God's Glory Bright"

Prayer of Confession

Assurance of Pardon

Children's Story . . . . "Rhoda"

Scripture . . . . Acts 15:1-2;
1 Corinthians 10:23-31;
Matthew 13:16-18, 31-33

Hymn . . . . "Wade in the Water"

Letter 1: Harriet Tubman

Hymn . . . . "Go Down Moses"
or "How Can I Keep from Singing"

Letter 2: Andre Trocme

Hymn . . . . "God of Grace
and God of Glory"

Letter 3: Mary Dyer

Silent Prayer

Letter 4: Martin Luther King, Jr.

Hymn . . . . "This Little Light of Mine"
or "Keep Your Eyes on the Prize"

Letter 5: Jakob Waldner

Hymn . . . . "We Are People
of God's Peace"

Sharing

Pastoral Prayer

Offering

Hymn of Commission . . . . "Help Us to
Help Each Other"

Benediction

Fellowship Meal

The Celebration

This celebration is based on the style of worship and fellowship in the early church. First-century congregations met in secret since their gatherings were illegal. They met in people's homes or in hidden places such as the catacombs. To simulate these settings, divide the congregation into groups of ten to thirty people and arrange for small groups to gather in individual homes or in separate rooms of the church. If meeting in homes, have one group meet in the church so that visitors and those who forget the unusual schedule will find a place to worship.

If these options are impossible, meet in the church as one congregation, but acknowledge through the bulletin or in the celebration that first-century gatherings would have been smaller and in private homes. For at least three Sundays in advance, inform the congregation of your plans.

Also, ahead of time, copy each of the readings (found in Resources for This Celebration) on separate sheets of paper, making a set for each group. Have the person in the group whose birthday is nearest the date of the celebration "secretly" deliver these letters to another group. Appoint the messenger at the beginning and send him or her on the errand early in the celebration. Each house church will hear a rap at the door during their worship and will let the messenger in to deliver the letters to the community. The letters will then be put aside until the proper time in the celebration.

Gather in Secret

You can further create a feeling of secrecy by meeting in basements, garages, barns, or dimly lit rooms. In any case, station someone at the door to admit people as they arrive. This "lookout" should have small sheets of paper on which he or she has drawn an arc. This was a code used by the early church to test whether a stranger was a believer. The stranger draws a second arc to create a fish, the anagram of Jesus' name, indicating that he or she also knows the secret code and should be allowed in. If someone doesn't know this practice, have the lookout explain.

Make a Sign

Give each person a small piece of poster board (about 2" or 5cm square). Have them cut two short pieces of heavy string or cord, dip them lightly in craft glue, and arrange them on the cardboard in the shape of a fish. Let dry for a few minutes. Then cover the square with aluminum foil, rubbing the surface firmly until the shape of the fish shows in relief. With a hot glue gun, attach a safety pin or jewelry clasp on the back of each one and wear it.

Hymn of Gathering

"What Is This Place?" (Smith/Huijbers)

Call to Worship

One: Hear, O Israel,

All: The Lord is our God, the Lord alone.

One: You shall love the Lord your God

All: with all your heart, with all your soul, with all your might.

One: Hear O sisters and brothers,

All: Jesus is Lord.

Invocation

Gracious God, we have repeated the words of the first-century Christians. May they not be empty words, but rather a part of our daily living. As we today reflect on those early years, give us new confidence that your church will stand. Help us to hear your word as we, your people, struggle with issues that confront the church today. Enable us to find our unity in you. Amen.

Hymns of Praise

"Shepherd of Eager Youth" (Clement of Alexandria) and "O Splendor of God's Glory Bright" (Ambrose of Milan)

Prayer of Confession

We confess, O God, our intolerance: we insist that others think as we do. We confess our impatience: we expect others to journey at our pace. We confess our arrogance: we want to make others into our image. In your graciousness, forgive us we pray. Amen.

Assurance of Pardon

Plainsong (See Resources for This Celebration.)

Children's Story

"Rhoda" (See Resources for This Celebration.)

Scripture

Acts 15:1-2; 1 Corinthians 10:23-31; Matthew 13:16-18, 31-33; Matthew 16:13-18

Hymn

"Wade in the Water" (African American spiritual)

Letters

When first-century Christians gathered, they would read letters of encouragement, admonishment, and instruction from church leaders. Throughout the history of the church, Christians have continued to hold the community of believers together with encouragement, admonishment, and instruction from brothers and sisters in the faith. Hear these letters from Christians who struggled under slavery, persecution, and controversy, and who formed and shaped the church (see Resources for This Celebration).

Letter 1: Harriet Tubman
Runaway Slave and Underground Railroad Engineer

Hymn

"Go Down Moses" (African American spiritual) or "How Can I Keep from Singing" or other spiritual

Letter 2: Andre Trocme
Pastor and Harborer of Jews During World War II

Hymn

"God of Grace and God of Glory" (Fosdick)

Letter 3: Mary Dyer
Quaker Leader and Martyr

Silent Prayer

In the Quaker style, allow people to offer sentence prayers if they are led by the Spirit.

Letter 4: Martin Luther King, Jr.
African American Pastor and Civil Rights Leader, 1963

Hymn

"This Little Light of Mine" (African American spiritual) or "Keep Your Eyes on the Prize" (African American spiritual)

Letter 5: Jakob Waldner
Hutterite, 1918

Hymn

"We Are People of God's Peace" (Simons/Horn)

Sharing

Provide reflection time and, in the style of the Society of Friends, allow people to speak about the issues that they believe most affect the church today. Encourage people to make statements rather than discuss or debate. During this time, pass out stamped postcards and invite people to write messages of encouragement to leaders of the church.

Worship Leader: Grace and peace to you from God our Saviour. It is with joy that I greet you and commend you for your faith and for your willingness to face the difficult issues of the church prayerfully and with love for one another.

Remember the period of our history when the question of whether or not new converts to Christianity had to first become Jews and observe Jewish customs and religious laws. At the time, Christian Jews attended synagogue and temple, celebrated the sabbath and all the festivals, observed the law in all of its detail as part of their joyous response to God. Then Paul and others began to witness to Gentiles. Great numbers confessed Jesus as Lord and Paul welcomed them into the fellowship without demanding circumcision and without demanding that they become Jews. Jewish and Gentile Christians formed one fellowship and ate at table together as equals and partners. This practice in Antioch was shocking to many Christian Jews in Jerusalem whose culture and faith already faced annihilation. It was a serious problem.

We have our own crises of faith and immovable barriers between brother and sister. In the next few minutes of reflection time, write a note of encouragement to the leaders of our church and, if you feel led, reflect aloud about the things that divide us and the hope for church.

Pastoral Prayer

Offering

Worship Leader: The new church stopped making burnt offerings because Jesus' great sacrifice on the cross made burnt offerings meaningless and unnecessary. Instead, Christians offered their very selves and their gifts to sustain the body of Christ, the church. Let us imitate our Lord, sacrificing deeply to enable Jesus' ministry to flourish.

Hymn of Commission

"Help Us to Help Each Other" (Wesley)

Benediction

Fellowship Meal

Sing the doxology as the table grace. Serve a potluck meal and involve adults and children in after-dinner games.

Resources for This Celebration

Assurance of Pardon
(Plainsong)

Hear the good news: when we con-fess

God cleans-es from un-right - eous - ness

For God is faith - ful, off - 'ring free

For - giv - ing grace to you and me.

Thanks ___ be to God. ___

Rhoda (based on Acts 12:12ff)

It was a very scary night. It happened a long time ago in a land far away from here. But it was so frightening that people still talk about it. In some countries of the world it could happen again! It was a very scary night. But right in the middle of everyone being so scared something funny happened. What a strange night!

It happened in the land of Palestine. Herod Agrippa was the head of the government. We might think of him as the president or the prime minister. He was the boss. He was going to make sure that there was no argument, no discussion, no disagreement, even if he had to be very cruel to keep things that way. When the Christians began to tell of Jesus and how Jesus said that God loves us all, Herod Agrippa became worried. He was afraid that if some people thought that Jesus was right and others thought that Jesus was wrong, there would be discussions and arguments and maybe even protesting in the streets. He would not allow that! So Herod Agrippa arrested those who talked about Jesus. He had a kind of public trial. Then he had the person beheaded.

Now you might think that people would not talk about Jesus any more. But those who loved Jesus just could not stop telling the good news that God loves us all. They gathered together in their homes in secret. They often came at night, slipping quietly along the darkened streets, coming at different times, making sure that no one followed them. They locked the doors. Then, softly they sang hymns and praised God and told the stories that Jesus had told. One of the homes where they often met was Mary's home. Mary was the mother of Mark the missionary preacher. They used her home because it was very large. It had a vestibule with a door to the street, then a courtyard, and then the living part of the house. Here they did not have to sing so softly. Here they could not be heard. They could sing and pray and tell stories of Jesus.

On this scary night many people were at Mary's house. They had called a special prayer meeting. They were praying for Peter who was in prison. They knew that the next morning he would be put on display on the street and then he would be beheaded. What a terrible night. Peter was a preacher that they all knew and loved. They prayed that God would be with him.

Suddenly it happened.

A knock at the door. Everyone became very quiet. "Did Herod's police see us?" they wondered. "Did a passing policeman hear us singing? Will they try to kill us all?"

Knock. Knock. There it was again. Who could it be?

"Rhoda," Mary said to the young girl, "you go to the front door. You are so quiet on your feet and so little that you can peek through the tiny slot with your keen eyes. Go and find out who is there."

Without a sound Rhoda left the room. She slipped through the courtyard and into the vestibule as gently as a summer breeze. She crept up to the hidden peep hole. Before she could even look out, she heard the loud knock. Then she heard, "It's me. Let me in."

Rhoda knew that voice. It was Peter's voice. She ran back through the vestibule and through the courtyard. She burst into the room where everyone was sitting like cold stone statues—almost afraid to breathe. "Guess who it is," she cried. "It's Peter!"

"Shh. Quiet!" said James.

"You're crazy," said someone else. We are here praying for Peter because he is in prison. Tomorrow they will behead him. Your fright has made you crazy."

"It is Peter's voice. I know it is!" insisted Rhoda.

Guess what. It really was Peter. Finally they got their wits together and let Peter in before the prison guards caught up with him. Then how they laughed. They laughed at how Rhoda was so excited that she did not open the door for Peter. They laughed at how they were praying for Peter and then did not believe that God had answered their prayer.

They were so happy that they laughed and sang hymns and praised God long into the night. And they told each other that God would make sure that there would always be someone to tell the good news of God's love.

Letters

Letter 1. Harriet Tubman
Runaway Slave and Underground Railroad Engineer

The South was becoming inexorably more and more an armed camp. "Wanted" posters were everywhere with descriptions of fleeing slaves, above all of "Moses" [Harriet Tubman], the one who led out so many bands and who was believed by slave-owners to be a man. Harriet usually disguised herself by dressing as a man. She had gained the needed physical strength and stamina during years as a field hand when masters gladly allowed her her preference of field work over house work—and thus got a field hand labour for a woman's wages. But those in that male-dominated world who knew her best often compared her to Joan of Arc.

Steadily withdrawing the slaves from her Bucktown, Maryland, home area, Harriet caused the value of slaves in markets there to drop dramatically. Owners refused to pay large amounts, knowing there was little certainty of keeping the slaves. The rewards offered for the capture or death of Moses was set at a total of $40,000.

Harriet Tubman is considered to have been the most successful of the underground engineers. Only the most committed, usually Blacks, were willing to take on this dangerous role. Of the other engineers, many were captured and imprisoned, killed, or emotionally scarred if they survived. Her strength of spirit and ability to encourage and inspire those who followed her, her depth and richness of personality remain a source of wonder. She drew on dreams, visions, and intuitions. Upon meeting John Brown, she identified him as a man she had seen in a dream. Twice she went to an abolitionist who received money for her from European supporters and told him how much he was holding and that she had come to collect it. Three years before the Emancipation Proclamation, she had a vision of the freedom of her people. Then at the time of its pronouncement she said, "I rejoiced all I could then; I can't rejoice no more."

Harriet attributed these dreams, warnings, and the like, to God. Her unshakable confidence and faith in God's love and providence were manifested often along the railroad and later during the War Between the States. In both circumstances she was certain of God's care; she believed that she would die only at the appointed and right moment, then to be welcomed by God. When asked how she could go back into danger knowing the price on her head, she answered, "Why, don't I tell you, ''twasn't me 'twas THE LORD.' I always told him, 'I trust to you. I don't know where to go or what to do, but I expect you to lead me,' and he always did."

By Maggie Fisher, excerpted
from *The Universe Bends
Toward Justice*, p. 81.

Letter 2. Andre Trocme
Pastor and Harbourer of Jews During World War II

Basic truth has been taught to us by Jesus Christ. What is it? The person of any one man is so important in the eyes of God, so central to the whole of his creation, that the unique, perfect being, Jesus, (a) sacrificed his earthly life for that one man in the street, and (b) sacrificed his perfection [by taking the blame for his sins] in order to save that single man. Salvation has been accomplished without any regard to the moral value of the saved man.

From "The Law Itself Was a Lie"
Fellowship, January 1955, p. 4.

Letter 3. Mary Dyer
Quaker Leader and Martyr

In September of 1659 two English Quakers, William Robinson and Marmaduke Stephenson, went to Boston, taking with them an eleven year old girl, Patience Scott. The two men were thrown in jail and the child closely confined in the home of the governor. Mary Dyer [a Quaker woman], decided she must go and bring the girl home. She had a stormy interview with Governor Endicott, who formally banished her once and for all from the colony. Stephenson and Robinson were also banished. They left, but in less than a month all three were back. On October 19, the General Court sentenced them to death by hanging.

The execution was set for October 27. The three Quakers were uplifted rather than depressed by their sentence and spent their time in prayer and meditation. Each of them was furnished with writing materials so that they could write a final letter to their families. Mary Dyer decided to make an appeal to the governor not for her own life, but to save him and his magistrates from the crime they were about to commit.

"In love and meekness I beseech you to repeal these cruel laws, to stay this wicked sentence. Though you have harmed us grievously, in the past, no life has been lost. But now, if you shed our innocent blood you will kill not only our bodies, but your infinitely more precious souls. For the wages of sin is death, and 'tis a heinous sin indeed to kill your fellowmen, children of God like you, who only seek to preach his Word. Relent, I beg you, repent I implore you, for if you persist you will surely feel God's heavy hand on Judgement Day. . . .

"Therefore, let the light of Christ with its loving warmth soften your hearts and let the light bring your minds out of darkness to freedom and glory, for his is the way to everlasting life."

On the day of the execution, the three walked to the gallows hand in hand. Mary Dyer told one of the magistrates that this was the hour of greatest joy she had ever experienced. "No ear can hear, nor tongue utter, and no heart understand the sweet incomings and refreshings of the Spirit of the Lord which I now feel."

Mary Dyer's joy was short lived, however. She climbed the gallows with her companions and the hangman covered her eyes with a cloth, bound her legs and arms, and placed the rope around her neck. The other two went cheerfully to their deaths, but when it was her turn a court officer raced up with a last minute reprieve. The authorities feared the effect on public opinion of hanging a woman, and had planned this stratagem all along, hoping to frighten Mary Dyer into submission. Her eyes were unbound, her arms and legs freed, and the crowd cheered and urged her to step down from the gallows. She argued that she did not want to live unless the bloody laws were repealed, but it was of no use. Her husband was waiting at the foot of the gallows with a swift horse to take her home again and, heartbroken, she acquiesced.

. . . All along she had felt that she must return to Boston, "to look their bloody laws in the face." In May of 1660 she set out with two fellow Quakers. She was immediately arrested and brought once more before Governor Endicott, who once more sentenced her to death.

. . . Some persecution of Quakers continued for another twenty years, but public opinion swung more and more strongly against it, and Mary Dyer's famous words on the occasion of her first trip to the gallows were remembered.

"But if one of us must die that the others may live, let me be the one, for if my life were freely granted by you, I could not accept it as long as my sisters suffered and my brothers died.

For what is life compared to the witness of Truth?"

By Margaret Hope Bacon, from *The Universe Bends Toward Justice*, pp. 11-12.

Letter 4. Martin Luther King, Jr.
African American Pastor and Civil Rights Leader, 1963

My dear fellow clergymen,

. . . I am in Birmingham because injustice is here. Just as the eighth-century prophets left their little villages and carried their "thus saith the Lord" far beyond the boundaries of their hometowns, and just as the Apostle Paul left his little village of Tarsus and carried the gospel of Jesus Christ to practically every hamlet and city of the Graeco-Roman world, I too am compelled to carry the gospel of freedom beyond my particular hometown. Like Paul, I must constantly respond to the Macedonian call for aid.

. . . But as I continued to think about the matter [of being in jail for conscience's sake], I gradually gained a bit of satisfaction from being considered an extremist. Was not Jesus an extremist in love—"Love your enemies, bless them that curse you, pray for them that despitefully use you." Was not Amos an extremist for justice—"Let justice roll down like waters and righteousness like a mighty stream." Was not Paul an extremist for the gospel of Jesus Christ—"I bear in my body the marks of the Lord Jesus." Was not Martin Luther an extremist—"Here I stand; I can do none other so help me God." Was not John Bunyan an extremist— "I will stay in jail to the end of my days before I make a butchery of my conscience." Was not Abraham Lincoln an extremist— "This nation cannot survive half slave and half free." Was not Thomas Jefferson an extremist— "We should hold these truths to be self-evident, that all men are created equal." So the question is not whether we will be extremist but what kind of extremist will we be? Will we be extremists for hate or will we be extremists for love? Will we be extremists for the preservation of injustice—or will we be extremists for the cause of justice? In that dramatic scene on Calvary's hill, three men were crucified. We must not forget that all three were crucified for the same crime—the crime of extremism. Two were extremists for immorality, and thusly fell below their environment. The other, Jesus Christ, was an extremist for love, truth, and goodness, and thereby rose above his environment. So, after all, maybe the South, the nation, and the world are in dire need of creative extremists.

I hope this letter finds you strong in the faith. I also hope that circumstances will soon make it possible for me to meet each of you, not as an integrationist or a civil rights leader, but as a fellow clergyman and a Christian brother. Let us all hope that the dark clouds of racial prejudice will soon pass away and the deep fog of misunderstanding will be lifted from our fear-drenched communities and in some not too distant tomorrow the radiant stars of love and brotherhood will shine over our great nation with all of their scintillating beauty.

Yours for the cause of Peace and Brotherhood,

Martin Luther King, Jr.

From "Letter from a Birmingham Jail," in *The Universe Bends Toward Justice*, pp. 171-184.

Letter 5. Jakob Waldner
Hutterite, 1918

Today they called us to the office individually and asked whether we would clean the hospital yard. Of the Hutterites, only the two Entz brothers were asked. At 1 p.m., they called us together again and we walked two by two to the hill. Peter Tschetter and I were at the head of the group. Thinking that this was supposed to be another march, we decided to go only far enough to see where it was leading. Then we discovered a major standing there on the hillside, who gathered around him about one hundred of us in a semicircle.

He made the following speech: "You are all registered soldiers according to the law. President Wilson is the highest authority in the United States. It has taken him six months to find noncombatant tasks for you. If you refuse now, you must know that you can be punished by death or life imprisonment in a penitentiary. Don't be such fools as to let this happen to you. Even a Christian can drive a car or take care of the sick or do something else. And now forget that I am a major and that you are soldiers and let us discuss this as friends. I am speaking today as the spokesman of our highest Army chief. If anyone has anything to say, let him speak freely."

After that, one man by the name of Moler stood up and said the following: "I beg your pardon for having to disagree with you, but you and I are two kinds of people. I am Christian-minded and you are worldly-minded. You cannot understand the situation as well as I can, and I don't hold this against you. I have given myself to God on my knees, and he is the judge over the whole world. We must obey him more than men. I now want to give a parable since you think that a Christian can help in the war without guilt. If one man buys powder or other explosive material, a second man transports the dynamite to the bridge, a third man sets the explosive, and the fourth man blows up the bridge, then tell me: Whom will the government arrest and punish? Only the fourth man, or all four of them?"

The major did not know what to reply and therefore said without thinking: "None of the men would be punished for this is wartime."

"Yes," Moler said, "if this were done to the enemy, the men would be praised for it."

The major left, quite bothered that he had made a slip. Thirteen signed their names for work in the camp and hospital. Today the major understood everything that we had to say. We were called five times today. May God continue to protect us as He has to the present. Amen.

Readings from *Mennonite Writings*, pp. 136-137.

Resources

Books

A World At Prayer: The New Ecumenical Prayer Cycle. Mystic, Conn.: Twenty-Third Publications, 1989.

Appleton, George. *Jerusalem Prayers for the World Today*. London, England: Society for Promoting Christian Knowledge, 1989.

Aschliman, Kathryn, Ed. *Growing Toward Peace*. Scottdale, Pa.: Herald Press, 1993.

Banquet of Praise: A Book of Worship Resources. Washington, D.C.: Bread for the World, 1990.

Burstein, Chaya M. *The Jewish Kids Catalog*. Philadelphia, Pa.: The Jewish Publication Society of America, 1983.

Costello, Elaine, illus. *Religious Signing*. Toronto, Ont.: Bantam Books, 1986.

DeSola, Carla. *The Spirit Moves: A Handbook of Dance and Prayer*. Austin, Tex.: The Sharing Company, 1986.

Festival: Worship with Jesus, Worship Today. Nashville, Tenn.: Cokesbury, 1992.

Fry-Miller, Kathleen; Judith Myers-Walls; and Janet Domer-Shank. *Peace Works*. Elgin, Ill.: Brethren Press, 1989.

Fry-Miller, Kathleen, and Judith Myers-Walls. *Young Peacemakers Project Book*. Elgin, Ill.: Brethren Press, 1988.

Gerber, Suella; Kathleen Jansen; and Rosemary Widner. *Becoming God's Peacemakers*. Newton, Kan.: Faith and Life Press, 1992.

In Spirit and in Truth: A Worship Book. Geneva, Switzerland: WCC Publications, 1991.

Luvmour, Sambhova and Jasette. *Everyone Wins! Cooperative Games and Activities*. Philadelphia, Pa.: New Society Publishers, 1990.

MacKenthun, Carole, and Paulinus Dwyer. *Peace*. Carthage, Ill.: Shining Star Publications, 1986.

Milen, Teddy. *Kids Who Have Made a Difference*. Northampton, Mass.: Pittenbruach Press, 1989.

Schlabach, Joetta Handrich. *Extending the Table: A World Community Cookbook*. Scottdale, Pa.: Herald Press, 1991.

Weaver, Judy. *Celebrating Holidays and Holy Days in Church and Family Settings*. Nashville, Tenn.: Discipleship Resources, 1989.

With All God's People: The New Ecumenical Prayer Cycle. Geneva, Switzerland: WCC Publications, 1989.

Zimmerman, Martha. *Celebrate the Feasts.* Minneapolis, Minn.: Bethany House, 1981.

Music

Hymnal: A Worship Book
Brethren Press
1451 Dundee Avenue
Elgin, IL 60120
800 441-3712
or
Faith & Life Press
Box 347
Newton, KS 67114-0347
800 743-2484
or
Mennonite Publishing House
616 Walnut Avenue
Scottdale, PA 15683-1999
800 245-7894

Jewish Liturgical Music
Purple Pomegranate Productions
80 Page Street
San Francisco, CA 94102

Teaching Peace (audiocassette) by Red Grammar
The Children's Bookstore Distribution
67 Wall Street, Suite 2411
New York, NY 10005

Videos

EcuFilm (an ecumenical film/video distribution service)
810 Twelfth Avenue South
Nashville, TN 37203
800 251-4091

Shalom Lifestyles (youth video curriculum)
Mennonite Media Productions
1251 Virginia Ave.
Harrisburg, VA 22801-2497
800 999-3534